ExcelTips

Excel 2003 Graphics and Charts

Second Edition

Compiled from the pages of ExcelTips, *your free weekly productivity newsletter*

tips.NET

Excel 2003 Graphics and Charts

Published by:

Sharon Parq Associates, Inc.
PO Box 794
Orem, UT 84059

For information on purchasing, distributing, or reselling books published by Sharon Parq Associates, Inc., please visit our website (www.SharonParq.com) or call 801-607-2035. Our books are also available through select online resellers such as Amazon.com.

ISBN: 978-1-61359-035-5 (e-book on CD-ROM)
ISBN: 978-1-61359-036-2 (e-book)
ISBN: 978-1-61359-037-9 (printed book)

Produced and published in the United States of America

Revision history:

17 Jun 2009: First published
1 Jun 2011: Second edition

Table of Contents

Introduction

Many people, especially when they are new to Excel, create worksheets that contain only numbers, text, and formulas. Excel worksheets can contain much more than these elemental items. You can add all sorts of graphics to your worksheets or you can create amazing charts from your data. These items—graphics and charts—can liven up your data and provide some exciting ways to make your information mean even more.

Excel provides a variety of tools that you can use to insert graphics, modify those graphics, make them look exactly the way you want, and then print them out. Closely related to working with graphics, Excel gives you the ability to create dozens of types of charts, adjust their appearance in excruciating detail, and print those masterpieces.

There are many advantages to the graphics and charting power provided, chief of which is that you can use Excel's tools to create just about anything you can imagine. While nobody would claim that Excel is an adequate substitute for a dedicated graphics program, its tools can meet most day-to-day graphics needs—especially when it comes to presenting or augmenting your data. In short, Excel's graphics and charting power can help you present your data in a more understandable, accessible manner.

Along with the advantages there is one major disadvantage—the capabilities of Excel's tools can be a bit confusing. While you might be able to imagine what you want to do with either graphics or charting, figuring out how to use the tools to implement what you've imagined can be daunting.

That's where ***Excel 2003 Graphics and Charts*** can benefit you. This second edition provides plenty of information about both graphics and charts, but it is not the dry, lifeless information you'll often find in computer books. Instead you'll find lots of implementation help and hands-on examples, along with the necessary background information.

Brought to you by the publisher of ***ExcelTips,*** your free weekly productivity newsletter, ***Excel 2003 Graphics and Charts*** focuses on what you need to know to understand and put graphics and charts to work right away. You'll discover ways to stretch your knowledge and enhance how you can present the data in your worksheets.

The information presented in ***Excel 2003 Graphics and Charts*** is organized into a collection of bite-sized "tips" that have appeared in various issues of ***ExcelTips.*** But there is more, because some of the information contained here has never appeared in any issue of ***ExcelTips.*** You get the most up-to-date and complete information available anywhere.

A Word about Versions

Common versions of Excel in use today (on Windows-based systems) are Excel 97, Excel 2000, Excel 2002, Excel 2003, Excel 2007, and Excel 2010. Given that the name of this e-book is ***Excel 2003 Graphics and Charts,*** you might be questioning if this e-book will work with the version of Excel you use.

In a word, it should. The instructions and screen shots used in this e-book were all created on an Excel 2003 system, but that shouldn't stop the information from being of use to you if you are using an older version. As you compare what is on your screen with what you see in this e-book, don't be surprised if there are small, cosmetic differences. If you run across discrepancies of a more serious nature (I don't think you will), I'd love you to e-mail me with the details. Send your message to allen@sharonparq.com.

There is, however, one group of Excel users who will not find the information in this e-book that useful: those who have taken the plunge and updated to either Excel 2007 or Excel 2010. The user interface in these latest versions is completely different than in earlier versions, and that goes for the tools related to graphics and charts. If you are an Excel 2007 or Excel 2010 user, check at the

Tips.Net store and you can find a version of this e-book that will work better for your purposes.

Need More Tips?

If you want to stay in top Excel form, consider subscribing to ***ExcelTips***. Your subscription is free; all you need is an e-mail account and you can receive a weekly dose of tips related to Excel. To subscribe, just visit the ***ExcelTips*** Web site:

http://excel.tips.net

ExcelTips is part of the Tips.Net network, a collection of websites designed to bring you helpful tips, tricks, and ideas that can save you time, effort, and money. You can see the full breadth of the Tips.Net network by visiting our website:

http://www.tips.net

Sharing this E-Book

There was a lot of work that went into putting this e-book together. That means that this information has value, and your friends, neighbors, and co-workers may want to share it.

The information in this e-book is copyrighted. Please do not share this information with others—you purchased ***Excel 2003 Graphics and Charts*** and you have a right to use it on your system. Another person who has not purchased this e-book does not have that right. It is the sales of this valuable information that makes the continued publishing of ***ExcelTips*** possible. If enough people disregard that simple economic fact, the newsletter will no longer be viable or available.

If you work for a company and your company purchased this e-book, remember that they purchased it for you. Just because a company purchases an e-book does not give the company the right to share that e-book with all their employees. (Think about it—does purchasing a book at the bookstore give the company the right to photocopy it for each of their employees? No, it does not.)

If your friends and coworkers think this information is valuable enough to ask you for it, they should think it is valuable enough to purchase on their own. After all, the price is low enough that just about anyone should be able to afford a copy.

It should go without saying that you cannot post this e-book or the information it contains on any electronic bulletin board, Web site, FTP site, newsgroup, or … well, you get the idea. The only place from which this e-book should be available is the ***ExcelTips*** Web site. If you want an original copy, visit the Tips. Net store at the following address:

http://store.tips.net

1

Adding Graphics to Worksheets

Inserting a Picture in Your Workbook

Excel allows you to insert a wide range of picture (graphic) types in your documents. You can insert the following types:

Picture Type	Filename Extension
Compressed Enhanced Metafile	EMZ
Compressed Macintosh PICT	PCZ
Compressed Windows Metafile	WMZ
Computer Graphics Metafile	CGM
CorelDraw	CDR
Encapsulated PostScript	EPS
Enhanced Metafile	EMF
FPX Format	FPX
Graphics Interchange Format	GIF
JPEG Format	JPG
Kodak Photo CD	PCD
Macintosh PICT	PCT
PC Paintbrush	PCX
Picture It! Format	MIX
Portable Network Graphics	PNG
Tagged Image File Format	TIF

Picture Type	Filename Extension
Windows Bitmap	BMP
Windows Metafile	WMF
WordPerfect Graphics	WPG

This list looks very inclusive, but you may not be able to insert all of these on your particular version of Excel. The graphic files you can actually import depends on the version of Excel you have installed and which import filters you installed.

To insert a picture in your workbook, follow these steps:

1. Choose Picture from the Insert menu, and then choose the From File option. This displays a file selection dialog box.
2. In the Files of Type field, select the type of graphics file you want to insert.
3. Locate and choose a filename for the picture you want to insert.
4. Click on Insert.

Excel inserts the picture as if it is floating over your worksheet. You can then move the picture by simply using the mouse to drag the picture a new location.

Inserting from a Camera or Scanner

You would be right to never consider Excel as a graphics program—it's not one, by any stretch o the imagination. However, Excel does provide some tools normally associated with graphics programs. One such tool is one that allows you to import a graphic image from either a camera or a scanner. Choose Insert | Picture | From Scanner or Camera. Excel shows what devices are available and you can select how you want the image imported.

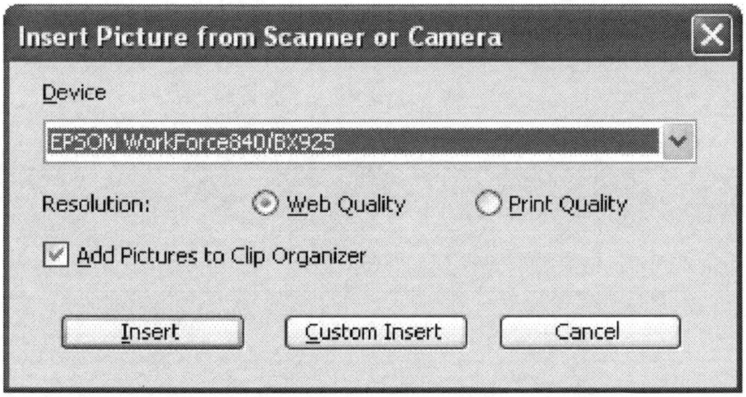

The Insert Picture from Scanner or Camera dialog box.

In reality, inserting pictures in this way works only if the camera or scanner is a TWAIN device. TWAIN is a protocol that allows images to be communicated from a source device (the camera or scanner) to a target device (in this case, Excel). For it to work properly, your scanner or camera must have the proper TWAIN drivers installed on your system.

Most scanners come with TWAIN drivers, but a growing number of today's digital cameras do not. Instead, the non-TWAIN cameras connect to a PC via a USB connector, and are then seen by Windows as just another disk drive accessible from the computer. If your camera uses a USB connection you can insert a picture by choosing Insert | Picture | From File and selecting the picture from the camera itself.

Putting a Graphic in a Header or Footer

Excel users have, for years, asked if there is a way to place graphics in headers or footers. Various methods have been devised to do just that, as discussed in other ***ExcelTips***. Users of Excel 2002 and Excel 2003 may be glad to know that it is even easier to add graphics to headers or footers. In fact, Microsoft added a direct capability to place graphics in headers or footers. Just follow these steps:

1. Choose Page Setup from the File menu. Excel displays the Page Setup dialog box.
2. Make sure the Header/Footer tab is selected.

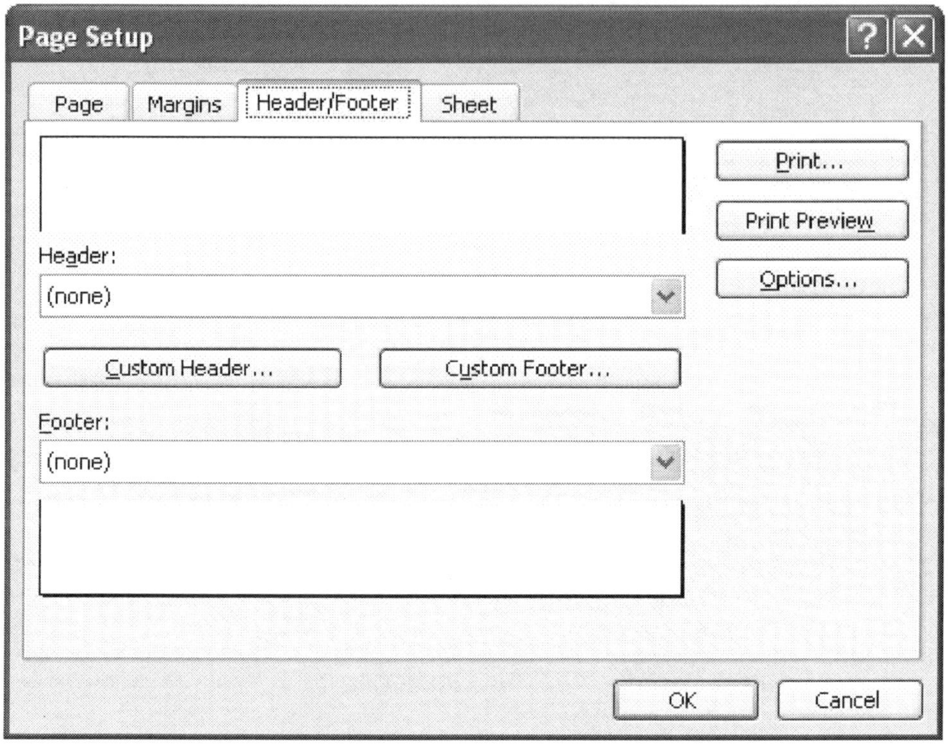

The Header/Footer tab of the Page Setup dialog box.

3. Click on the Custom Header or Custom Footer button, depending on which one you want to change. Excel displays either the Header or Footer dialog box.

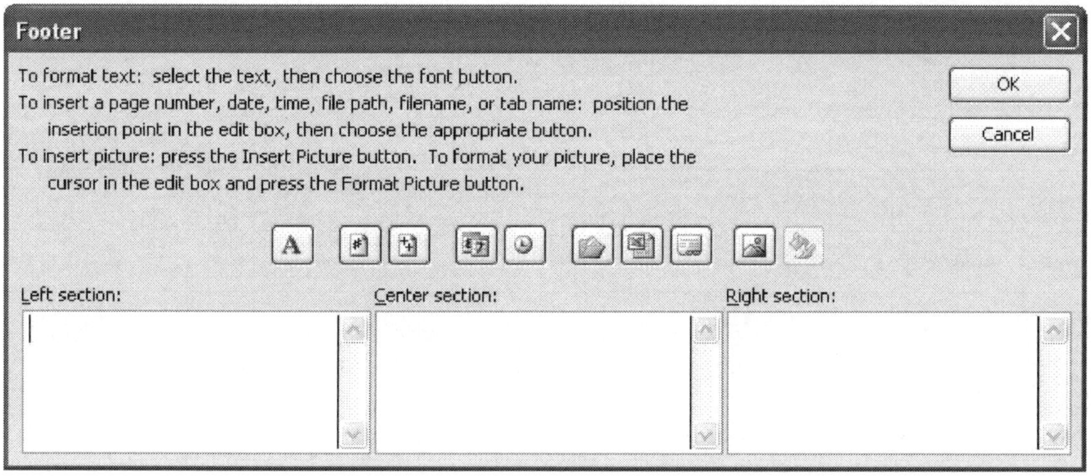

The Footer dialog box.

4. Select the section of the header or footer (left, center, or right) in which you want your graphic to appear.
5. Click on the Insert Picture button. It is the second button from the right. Excel displays the Insert Picture dialog box.
6. Use the controls in the dialog box to locate and select the graphic you want in the header or footer.
7. Click on Insert. Excel places the graphic at the designated spot in the header or footer, displaying the code &[Picture] where the graphic will appear.
8. Make other changes to the header or footer, as desired.
9. Click on the OK button to close the Header or Footer dialog box.
10. Click on OK to close the Page Setup dialog box.

Capturing a Screen

There may be times when you need to include a screen shot within your Excel worksheet. The easiest way to do this is as follows:

1. Set up your screen to look the way you want it to.
2. Press the **PRINTSCREEN** key. This copies the screen to the Clipboard.

3. Start Excel (if it is not already started) and select the cell closest to where you want the screen to appear.
4. Press **Ctrl+V** to paste the contents of the Clipboard.

This action results in the entire screen being pasted in your worksheet. If you wanted, instead, to only copy and paste a single dialog box or the active window, simply use **Alt+PrintScreen** in step 2.

If either of these methods still does not fit your needs (for instance, you want to include only a small part of the screen), you can use the following:

1. Set up your screen to look the way you want it to.
2. Press the **PrintScreen** key. This copies the screen to the Clipboard.
3. Start the Paint accessory (or some other graphics program) and maximize the screen.
4. Press **Ctrl+V** to paste the contents of the Clipboard into the program.
5. Use the program's editing tools to change the image as desired.
6. When complete, press **Ctrl+C** to copy the image to the Clipboard.
7. Start Excel (if it is not already started) and select the cell closest to where you want the screen to appear.
8. Press **Ctrl+V** to paste the contents of the Clipboard.

You should understand that once the screen is placed in your workbook, you can move and manipulate it the same as any other graphic. Also note that adding quite a few graphics to your worksheet can dramatically increase the size of the file in which your workbook is saved.

Taking a Picture

Excel provides a nifty little tool that allows you to create a picture from a range of cells, from a chart, or from another object in your worksheet. Follow these steps:

1. Select the cells or other object you want a picture of. (If you select cells, they must be contiguous.)
2. Hold down the **SHIFT** key as you click the Edit menu.
3. Choose Copy Picture. Excel displays the Copy Picture dialog box.

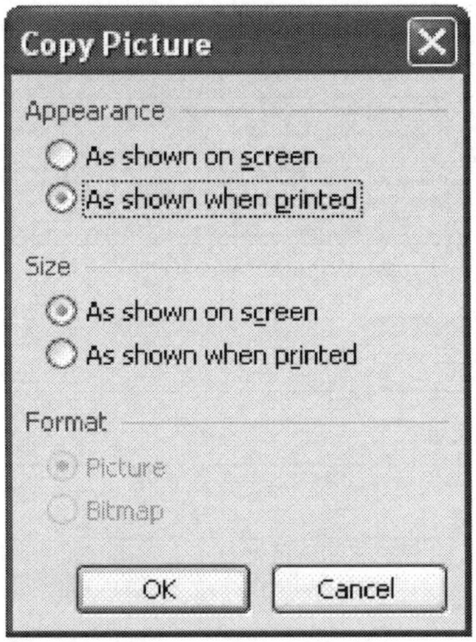

The Copy Picture dialog box.

4. In the top part of the dialog box, specify what you want in the picture.
5. In the bottom part of the dialog box, specify how you want the graphic saved.
6. Click OK.

The result is that you now have a graphic in the Clipboard—either a metapicture or a bitmap, depending on your choice in the bottom portion of the dialog box—that you can paste anywhere. Paste it in another workbook, paste it in an e-mail, or paste it in a Word document. You can paste it just about anywhere because it is no longer an Excel object, but an actual graphic.

You should know that if you choose "As Shown On Screen" in the Copy Picture dialog box, that doesn't mean that Excel copies the picture exactly as shown.

The copied picture will always be at a 100% zoom magnification, regardless of what zoom setting you are using. Thus, if you are viewing your worksheet at 125% zoom, take a picture of some cells, and then paste the picture back into the workbook, it will look smaller than the rest of your workbook does because of how the picture is capture.

Inserting Video into Worksheets

Excel allows you to add more to your workbooks than just numbers or text. You can also add all sorts of other objects. For instance, you can add simple graphics, pictures, or even videos. How you add graphics and pictures has been covered in other ***ExcelTips.*** Adding video is a horse of a different color, however.

Why is adding video different? The primary reason is because videos can be so huge. Consider the normal way to add objects:

1. Choose Object from the Insert menu. You will see the Object dialog box.
2. Click on the Create from File tab.

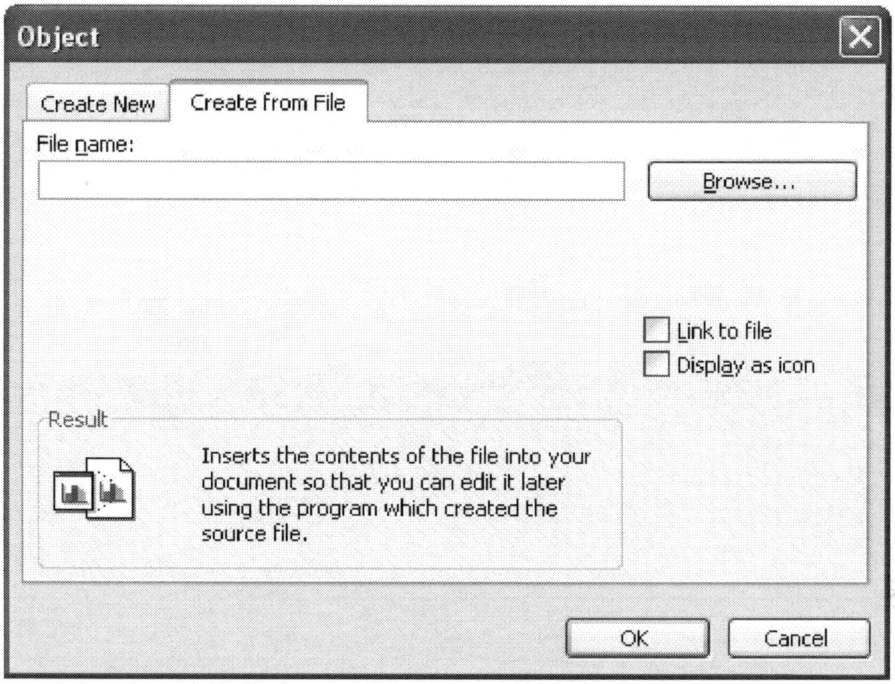

The Create from File tab of the Object dialog box.

3. Use the controls on the dialog box to locate the video file that you want.
4. Make sure the Display As Icon check box is selected.
5. Click on OK.

Did you notice that the Object dialog box had a check box that controlled whether the video would be linked or not? The default is for the video not to be linked, which means it will be embedded. Videos are notoriously huge, and the size of that video (however many megabytes or gigabytes it is) is added to your workbook when the video is embedded. This makes the workbook much harder to distribute to others.

You might think that the size issue can be solved by not embedding and, instead, linking to the video. While this does solve some issues, it raises others. When the video is linked, only the path to the file is stored in the document, but it is a fully qualified path. This means that, even if both documents are in the same directory, the directory name becomes part of the link. If you move both files or send them to someone else who stores them on their system, the link is automatically broken.

Another thing to keep in mind—regardless of whether you link or embed—is that if you share your workbook with others, they need to have a video player capable of playing the video you've added to the workbook.

A totally different approach is to simply hyperlink to your videos. You can either upload the videos to a video sharing service (such as YouTube) or you can put them on a local drive. Either way, a hyperlink is easy to add to your worksheet. Assuming that the video is something that can be played by your Web browser, the hyperlink could be a good route to go.

Creating an Organization Chart

One of the tools available in Excel is the ability to create organization charts. You do this by just choosing Diagram from the Insert menu. Excel displays the Diagram Gallery dialog box, which shows six different types of diagrams you can add to your worksheet. The default diagram type is Organization Chart. Click OK, and the chart appears in your worksheet as a graphic object.

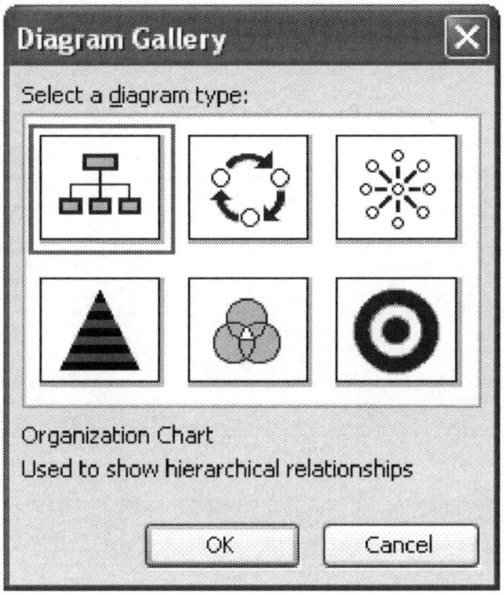

The Diagram Gallery dialog box.

Along with the actual organization chart, Excel displays the Organization Chart toolbar whenever the chart is selected. This toolbar allows you to add different boxes to the chart (using the Insert Shape drop-down menu), as well as to specify how the chart should be organized (using the Layout drop-down menu).

In Excel, organization charts are made up shapes and lines. Lines are automatically added or removed as you add or remove shapes. If you would like to change the formatting of any of the elements in the organization chart, right-click on the element and choose Format AutoShape from the Context menu.

2

Moving and Positioning Graphics

Selecting Drawing Objects

When you create a drawing in Excel, that drawing is made up of objects. The tools on the Drawing toolbar allow you to create both text and graphics objects, which can be moved and arranged in virtually any manner desired.

The first step is selecting an object. Selecting an object is virtually the same as in many other Windows programs. All you need to do is point at the object with the mouse and then click the mouse button. You can tell when an object has been selected because it is surrounded by small squares called ***handles***.

You can also build selection sets of objects. You do this by selecting the first object in the set, and then holding down the **Shift** key as you select each additional object. If you find you want to remove an object from your selection set, just hold down the **Shift** key and click your mouse on the object again.

Moving Drawing Objects

Over the course of many ***ExcelTips*** you have learned different ways to create objects using the drawing tools provided in Excel. If you later want to change the positioning of these objects, you can do so in this manner:

1. Using the mouse, point to the shape you want to move, and click on it. Excel places small squares or circles called ***handles*** around the shape.

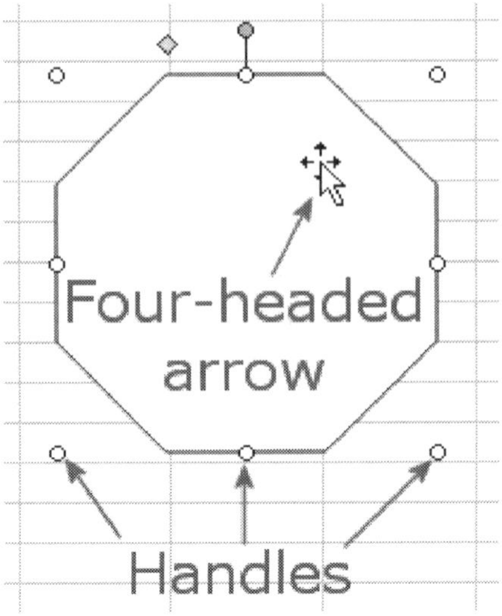

Moving a drawing object.

2. Using the mouse, point to the object. The mouse pointer should turn into a four-headed arrow.
3. Click and hold down the mouse button. Drag the object to the position desired.
4. Release the mouse button.

Nudging a Graphic

You already know that you can insert graphics in an Excel worksheet, and that you can position those graphics using the mouse. Sometimes using the mouse doesn't give the greatest amount of control over the placement of an object. For this reason, you may want to only use the mouse to handle the "rough placement" of a graphic. You can then nudge the graphic into its final location.

To nudge a graphic, simply make sure it is selected, and then use the arrow keys. Pressing an arrow key moves the graphic in the direction indicated. If you want even finer control, hold down the **Ctrl** key as you press an arrow key. The result is a nudge of a single pixel in the placement of the object. (Thus, if you want to nudge a graphic one pixel to the right, simply hold down the **Ctrl** key as you press the **Right Arrow** key.)

Sending Drawing Objects to the Back or Front

When you create objects in Excel using the Drawing toolbar, each object is drawn on its own layer. This means all objects are independent and can be moved on top of other objects. However, there may be times when you actually want an object to be under another object. You can do this by following these steps:

1. Select the pointer tool (the arrow) from the Drawing toolbar.
2. Using the mouse, point to the shape you want to send to the back, and click on it. Small square boxes called ***handles*** appear around the perimeter of the shape.
3. Choose Order from the Draw menu on the toolbar. Excel displays a set of ordering commands.
4. Choose the Send to Back option.

You can do the same sort of arrangement by choosing Bring to Front instead of Send to Back. Excel will move an item which may be behind others so that it overlays the others.

Specifying an Order for Drawing Objects

When you create drawing objects in Excel, each object is drawn on its own layer. This means all objects are independent and can be moved on top of other objects. This means that once you have drawn a number of different objects you can reorder them so that they appear in the order that you desire. You can do this by following these steps:

1. Select the pointer tool (the arrow) from the Drawing toolbar.
2. Using the mouse, point to the shape whose order you want to change. Small square boxes called handles appear at each corner in the shape.
3. Choose Order from the Draw menu on the toolbar. Excel displays a set of ordering commands.
4. Choose the ordering command that represents what you want to do.

You can also access the ordering commands by right-clicking on a drawing object and choosing Order from the resulting Context menu. There are four different ordering commands:

- **Bring to Front.** This option places the selected object on top of the layer stack, so it appears in front of any other objects.
- **Send to Back.** This option moves the selected object behind any other drawing objects.
- **Bring Forward.** This option simply moves the drawing object one step closer to the top of the layer stack.
- **Send Backward.** This option moves the drawing object one layer toward the bottom of the layer stack.

Positioning Graphics Evenly

Sometimes you may need to position graphics evenly within a worksheet. For instance, you may have four small graphics that will appear next to each other. You may want to make sure that the graphics are an equal distance from each other. To do this easily within Excel, follow these steps:

1. Using the mouse, roughly position the graphics where you want them to appear. You should make sure that the left-most graphic is where you want it, as is the right-most graphic.
2. Select all four graphics.
3. Make sure the Drawing toolbar is displayed.
4. Click on the Draw option on the Drawing toolbar, and then choose Align or Distribute.
5. Choose Distribute Horizontally from the resulting submenu. Excel positions the two inside graphics so that all four graphics are an equal distance from each other.

Grouping and Ungrouping Objects

Excel provides a feature found in many graphics programs—the ability to group graphics objects. For instance, you can spend a great deal of time positioning graphics objects in just the right position in order to achieve a desired effect. It is not unusual to create compound objects that are comprised of dozens of smaller objects.

Rather than risk getting the objects out of order or having their positions changed, you can ***group*** them so that they are treated as a single object. This is done by selecting all the objects you want grouped together (hold down the **SHIFT** key as you select each object).

Finally, choose the Group option which is available from the menu visible when you click on Draw on the Drawing toolbar. Notice that the individual handles for each object disappear, and instead, handles appear around a rectangle that encompasses all the objects in the group.

If you later want to ungroup the objects, simply choose the object you want to ungroup and choose Ungroup from the Draw menu.

3

Modifying and Formatting Graphics

Editing Graphics Objects

The technique you use to edit a graphics object depends on the type of object you are editing. The most common editing tasks—sizing and deleting objects—are easy to do in Excel.

To size an object, you first have to select it. This is done by using the mouse to point to one of the lines in the object. When you click on the mouse button, notice that handles appear around the outside of the rectangle that contains the object.

If you position the mouse pointer over one of the corner handles, it changes to a double-headed diagonal arrow. If you then click and hold down the mouse button, you can change the size of the object, keeping the proportions the same.

If you move the mouse pointer over one of the other handles, it changes to arrows that indicate the direction you can move the side. The shape of the graphics object is appropriately skewed, based on how you move the handle.

Finally, to delete a graphics object you need simply select it and press the **DEL** key. You can also use one of the delete options from the Edit menu.

Cropping Graphics

Once you place a graphic in your workbook, you may decide to crop it. Cropping means to cut off part of the graphic so it doesn't show in your workbook. To crop a graphic, follow these steps:

1. Make sure the Picture toolbar is visible. You can right click on the graphic and select Show Picture Toolbar if it is not.
2. Click on the Crop tool on the Picture toolbar.
3. Click on one of the graphic's corner or side markers with the mouse pointer.
4. Drag the marker towards the center of the graphic, stopping when you have cropped the desired amount.
5. You can turn off cropping by clicking on the Crop tool again or by pressing **Esc**.

You should understand that while cropping a graphic makes it look smaller, none of the original graphic is actually lost, it is only hidden. Cropping a graphic will not decrease the amount of storage space required by that graphic in your workbook.

Changing the Size of a Graphic

Excel allows you to easily resize a graphic you have placed in your workbook by following these steps:

1. Click on the graphic. A box appears around the object (this is designated by eight squares, or frame handles, around the outside of the graphic).
2. Use the mouse to point to one of the frame handles. Click on the left mouse button.
3. Drag the frame handle to resize the graphic.
4. Release the mouse button when the graphic is the size you want.

If you click and drag any of the four corner handles, then the proportions of the picture stay the same as you resize it. If you click and drag any of the other handles, the proportions of the picture are distorted.

Symmetric Resizing of Graphics

When you click on a graphic placed in your worksheet, eight selection handles appear around the object. These handles allow you to resize and crop the graphic in ways detailed in the previous tip.

One cool resizing feature is implemented if you hold down the **Ctrl** key while dragging one of the handles. Doing so causes Excel to symmetrically resize the image, adjusting not only the handle selected, but the handle opposite the one selected.

For instance, if you hold down the **Ctrl** key and drag the handle at the center of the right edge of the graphic inward by a half inch, then Excel also moves the left edge of the graphic inward by a half inch.

Making an Image Color Transparent

Whenever you place a picture in your worksheet, it is rectangular in nature. Sometimes, the image may actually be rather small, but the area occupied by the image is rather large. For instance, you could have a logo that is diagonal in nature, which means that there is a large "background area" on the image. This background area, for all intents and purposes, is wasted space.

Fortunately, Excel allows you to define a particular color in your image as a transparent color. This means you could select the background area of your image, designate it as transparent, and thereby allow the underlying cells show through. To make a transparent area in your image, follow these steps:

1. Select the image you want to modify.
2. The Picture toolbar should be visible. If it is not, use the Toolbars option from the View menu to turn on the Picture toolbar.

3. Click on the Set Transparent Color tool on the toolbar. (This is the second tool from the right.) The mouse cursor changes to look like the tool itself.
4. In the image, click on the color you want to be transparent.

If you can't select the Set Transparent Color tool in step 3, then you might not be able to set a transparent color in the image. Excel allows you to set the transparency color for bitmapped graphics, but not for other types. If you later want to turn off the transparency color, then you need to click the Reset Picture tool on the Picture toolbar.

Adding Drop Shadows

One helpful drawing tool you can use to format your drawings is known as the Shadow Style tool. Using this tool you can add a ***drop shadow*** behind an object. Adding drop shadows can help add more depth to your graphics, making them look like they are raised off the surface of the Excel worksheet.

To apply a drop shadow to an object you first select the object, then click on the Shadow Style tool. (It is very close to the right end of the Drawing toolbar.) Excel displays a number of different shadow types and positions. You can also modify the shadow, once placed, by choosing the Shadow Settings option. This displays a toolbar that allows you to adjust the characteristics of the shadow, without affecting the original object.

Hiding Graphics

If you are preparing worksheets that contain graphics, you may want to print the graphics on one version of the worksheet, but not print them on another. For example, you might be preparing a test for students, and the test requires them to draw a graph. You would want the printout of the student version of the test to leave space for drawing a graph, but the printout of the answer sheet should include the graphic showing how the students should answer.

The easiest way to handle this in Excel is to just turn off display of the graphics when you need to print the student test. In order to do this, create a single file that contains the questions and the answers. Assuming the answers are graphic files, follow these steps:

1. Choose Options from the Tools menu. Excel displays the Options dialog box.
2. Make sure the View tab is selected.

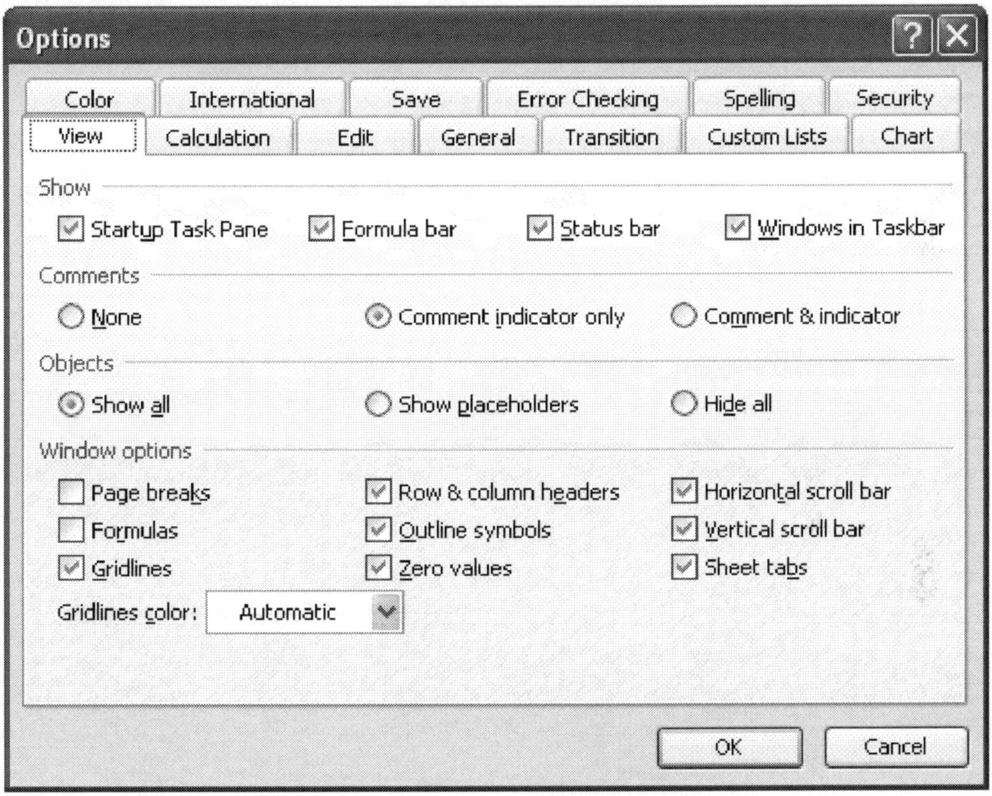

The View tab of the Options dialog box.

3. Make sure the Hide All radio button is selected.
4. Click on OK. The graphics disappear from the screen. (They are still there; they are simply invisible.)

You can now print your document, as normal. (Excel prints it very quickly since it doesn't need to send the graphics to the printer.) When you later want to see the graphics, repeat the steps, but make sure the Show All radio button is selected in step 3.

Resize Graphics Outside of Excel

As has been mentioned in other issues of ***ExcelTips,*** after inserting a graphic in your worksheet you can easily resize it to almost any size you want. While this can be easy to do, resizing graphics in this manner may not be the best approach to working with your graphics.

I've heard reports of people who have problems printing worksheets that have lots of graphics in them. Invariably, the root of the problem is graphics that are resized in Excel. Even if the graphic is only resized a few percentage points, it can still cause problems. Solving these types of problems can take quite a bit of trial and error and therefore a lot of time.

When you insert a graphic in Excel and then resize it, the full, large-scale graphic is still embedded within your worksheet. This adds to the overall size of your workbook and means it may be slower or more difficult for Excel to process.

Excel is not a graphics program. (Duh!) It makes sense that specialized graphics programs would be more adept at resizing and cropping graphics than what you can get when you use Excel. Therefore, you should consider resizing your graphics in a graphics program before placing them in a worksheet. Doing so may result in a higher-quality graphic in your worksheet, and it certainly will result in a lesser processing burden on Excel (not to mention a smaller workbook size).

If you are having problems printing graphics within Excel, consider resizing and processing the graphics outside of Excel completely using a program such as Paint Shop Pro or PhotoShop. Chances are good that you can solve your problems sooner than you think.

Protecting a Graphic

Larry asked if there was a way to protect a graphic inserted in a worksheet or the header or footer of a worksheet so that it cannot be removed. The answer (as with many things in Excel) is yes and no.

If you place a graphic in a worksheet, then when you protect the worksheet the graphic is also protected. In fact, once the worksheet is protected, you cannot even select any graphics in the worksheet, which is a prerequisite to them being deleted.

On the flip side of the coin, there is no way to protect graphics placed in headers or footers. Even if you protect the worksheet, the header and footer can still be changed, and thus the graphic can be selected and deleted.

Deleting All Graphics

Excel allows you to easily add graphics to a worksheet. This can be helpful, at times, but at other times you may want to delete all the graphics in a worksheet. The easiest way to delete all the graphics is to follow these steps:

1. Press **F5** to display the Go To dialog box.
2. Click on the Special button. Excel displays the Go To Special dialog box.

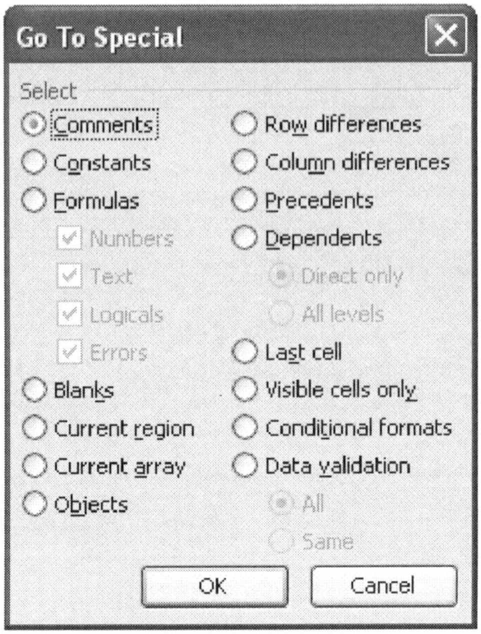

The Go To Special dialog box.

3. Make sure the Objects radio button is selected.
4. Click on OK. All the graphics in your worksheet are selected.
5. Press the **Del** key. All the graphics are deleted.

This solution works only if there are no other objects (besides graphics) in your worksheet. If you have other objects that you don't want deleted, then all you need to do is perform steps 1 through 4, and then hold down the **Ctrl** key as you use the mouse to click on each object you don't want deleted. When you are satisfied with the objects selected, finish up by following step 5.

Exporting a Graphics Group

It is not unusual to spend a good amount of time to get your Excel charts looking just the way you want them too. After putting in the time for the desired result, you may want to export a graphics group as a single GIF file so you can use it in other programs or on the Web.

Unfortunately, there is no way to do this in Excel. Even in VBA the group cannot be exported as a graphic. (Individual objects can, but not the group as a whole.) The only workaround that we could come up with seems rather old-fashioned. Follow these steps:

1. Display the worksheet containing the graphics group you want in the GIF file.
2. Make sure the Excel program window is maximized.
3. Choose Full Screen from the View menu. Excel hides many of its menus and toolbars.
4. Drag any stray toolbars to the side so that they don't obscure any portion of your graphics group.
5. Press the **PRINT SCREEN** key on your keyboard. The entire image of the screen is copied to the Clipboard.
6. Minimize or exit Excel.
7. Start your favorite graphics editing program. (My favorite is Paint Shop Pro.)
8. Paste the contents of the Clipboard into the graphics program.
9. Edit the graphic as desired, so that it contains only the grouped items.
10. Save the image as a GIF image.

4

Graphics and Your Data

Sorting with Graphics

You already know that Excel allows you to place graphics in your worksheets. You may not know, however, that Excel allows you to sort graphics along with the regular data in your tables. For instance, you could create an inventory table that has the requisite part numbers, descriptions, and quantities. You could also include a column that shows a small picture of each inventory item. When you later sort the table, the pictures sort right along with the rest of the data in the table.

If you can't seem to make the graphics sort along with the other data in the table, keep these pointers in mind:

- The graphics have to be sized so they fit completely within the cell. They cannot be taller or wider than the cell over which you placed them.
- You should make sure that the sorting function is selecting the column in which your graphics have been placed. You can check this by seeing if the column is selected when you choose the Sort option from the Data menu.

If your graphics still won't sort, the properties of the graphic may have been changed to prohibit sorting. Follow these steps:

1. Right-click on a graphic image. Excel displays a shortcut menu.
2. Choose Format Picture from the shortcut menu. Excel displays the Format Picture dialog box.
3. Make sure the Properties tab is selected.

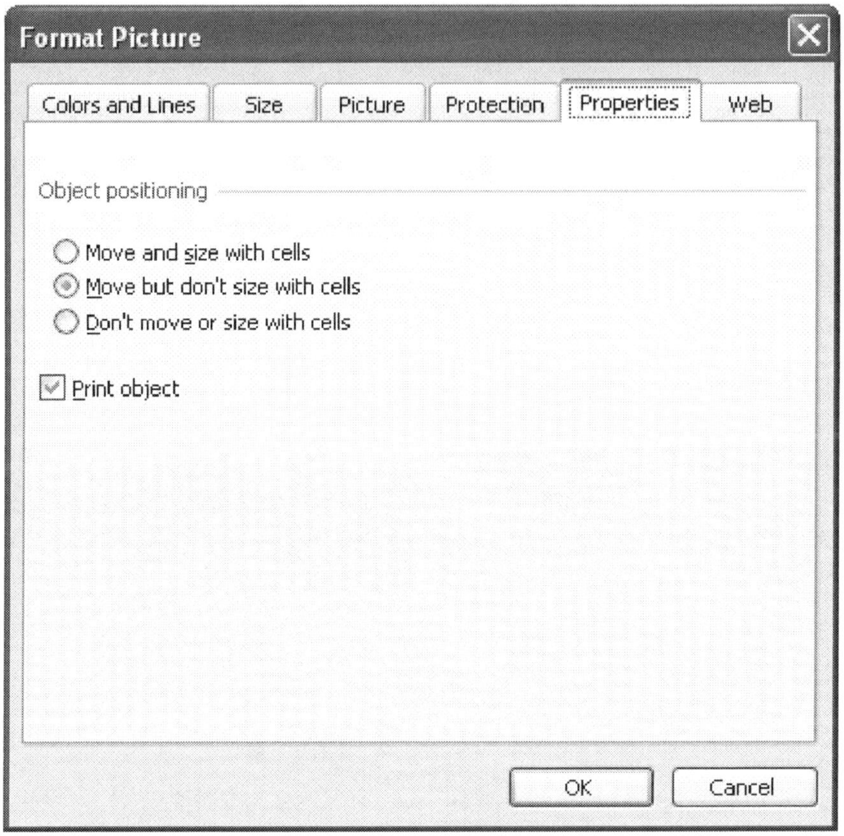

The Properties tab of the Format Picture dialog box.

4. Make sure the Don't Move or Size with Cells option is not selected.
5. Click on OK.
6. Repeat steps 1 through 5 for all the graphics in the column.

Displaying Images based on a Result

Dave has a large database that he keeps in an Excel workbook. It consists of material samples and uses the VLOOKUP function to generate various forms and reports. Dave wants to include a bitmap image on the form that changes according to one of the variables. For instance, if the form is describing an apple, then Dave wants a picture of an apple to appear; if describing a pear, then a pear should appear; and so on.

This is certainly a challenging task, but it is one that can surprisingly be done without macros. The steps are involved, but not that difficult to perform once you get to it:

1. On a new worksheet, select a cell (such as cell B4).
2. Enter the name "apple" into the Name box. This defines the name "apple" to refer to cell B4.
3. With cell B4 still selected, choose Insert | Picture | From File. Select the picture of the apple and insert it.
4. Enlarge the width and height of cell B4 so that the picture of the apple is contained entirely within the cell.
5. Repeat steps 1 through 4 for each of your other pictures, placing each picture in a different cell and naming them according to the contents of the picture. (For the sake of this example, I'll assume that "pear" is cell D4 and "orange" is cell F4.)
6. On the worksheet that will contain your form, create a formula that will contain the names of the fruit, such as the following formula, which displays "apple," "pear," or "orange," depending on the value in cell G1:

   ```
   =IF(G1=1,"apple",IF(G1=2,"pear",IF(G1=3,"orange","")))
   ```

   It is important that the formula reference the names exactly as you defined them in step 2 for each fruit's picture. For the sake of this example, I'll assume that you entered this formula in cell A1 of Sheet1.
7. Choose Name from the Insert menu, then choose Define. Excel displays the Define Name dialog box.

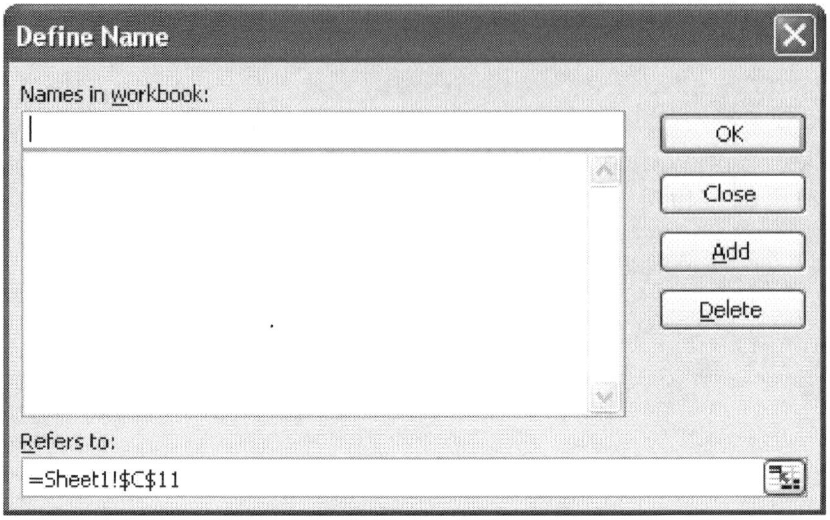

The Define Name dialog box.

8. Replace the contents of the Names In Workbook box with the word "Picture".
9. Replace the contents of the Refers To box with the following formula:

```
=INDIRECT(Sheet1!$A$1)
```

10. Click the OK button. You've now defined the name "Picture" to contain the formula entered in step 9.
11. On the worksheet that will contain your form, select the cell where you want the dynamic image to appear.
12. Choose Insert | Picture | From File. Select and insert a picture (it doesn't matter which one).

13. Make sure the picture you inserted in step 12 is selected.
14. In the formula bar, enter the formula **=Picture**. (This is the name you defined in steps 7 through 10.) The picture should change to reflect whatever fruit is named in cell A1.

Now, whenever the fruit name in cell A1 changes (which is, in turn, based on the value in cell G1), the image will change.

Hiding Graphics when Filtering

James has a worksheet that has graphics on top of cells that explain what is in the cells. The graphics sort with the cells just fine, but when he applies filters to the cells, the graphics bunch up at top of cells that are visible. James wonders if there is a way to have graphics hide when filtering data within cells.

The answer has to do with how you have the properties for the graphics set up. You need to make sure that the graphics are set to resize when the row height changes. Here's what you do:

1. Select the graphic (or graphics) whose properties you want to modify.
2. Right-click the graphic (or graphics). Excel displays a Context menu.
3. Choose Format Picture from the Context menu. Excel displays the Format Picture dialog box.
4. Make sure the Properties tab is displayed.

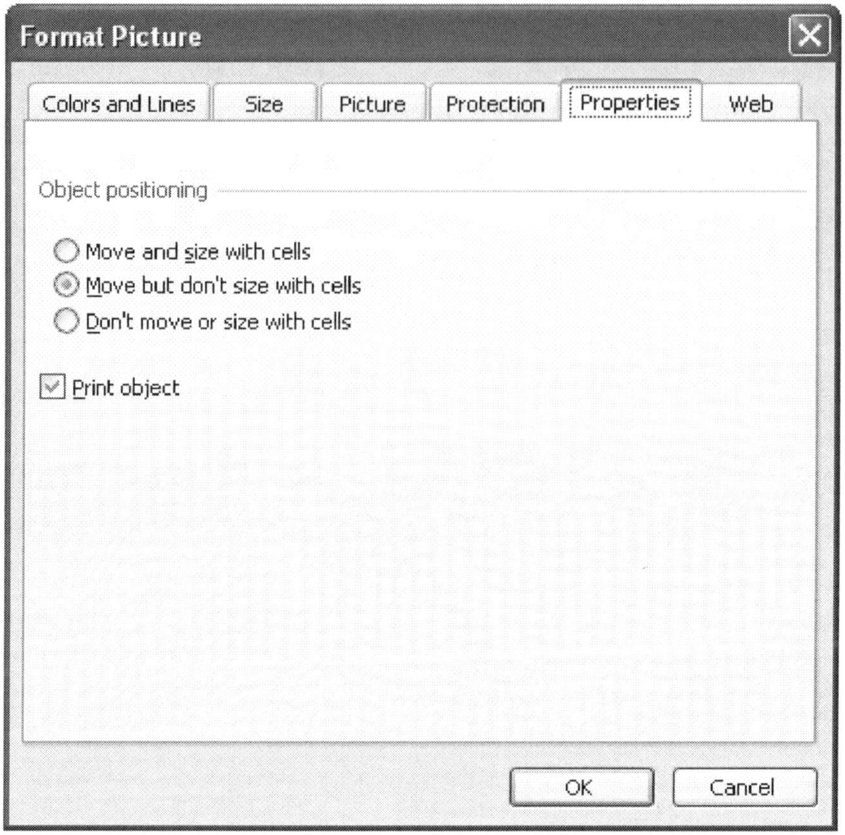

The Properties tab of the Size and Properties dialog box.

5. Make sure the Move and Size with Cells check box is selected.
6. Click OK.

It is step 5 that does the trick here. Since your graphics are sorting properly when you sort the worksheet, chances are good that you had the Move but Don't Size with Cells check box selected. This is what caused the graphics to bunch up—they couldn't resize when filtering hid the rows with which they were associated.

Deleting Graphics when Deleting a Row

Sethuraman has a worksheet where column A contains names, column B contains addresses, and column C contains a photo of the person. If he deletes the row, the photo remains. He wonders how the photo can be deleted at the same time the row is deleted.

This happens because of the way that the properties for the graphics are set up. If the only graphics in the worksheet are those for the people, then start by selecting all the graphics. (Press **F5**, click Special, select Objects, click OK.) Then, follow these steps to set the properties for all the selected graphics:

1. Right-click one of the graphics. Excel displays a Context menu.
2. Choose either Format Picture or Size and Properties from the Context menu, depending on your version of Excel. Excel displays either the Format Picture or Size and Properties dialog box.
3. Make sure the Properties tab is displayed.

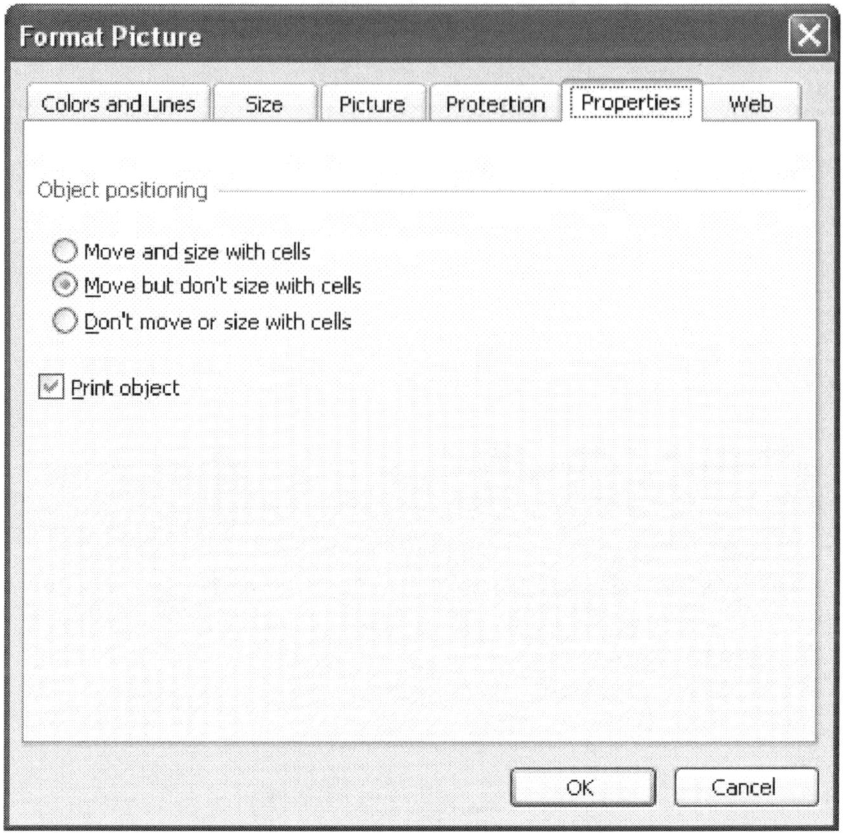

The Properties tab of the Size and Properties dialog box.

4. Make sure the Move and Size with Cells check box is selected.
5. Click OK.

Getting Rid of Fixed Objects

Peter has a filtered worksheet. When he takes all the filters off a message box pops up saying "Fixed objects will move!" There is no option other than clicking OK. Peter wonders what fixed objects are and how he can get rid of them.

"Fixed objects" can refer to a multitude of items, such as comments, graphics, controls, etc. They are considered "fixed" because they are placed in a spot on the worksheet and then Excel tries to keep them in that spot.

You can select the objects in a worksheet by pressing F5 to display the Go To dialog box, and then clicking Special. In the resulting dialog box click the Objects radio button and click OK. At this point all the objects are selected and you can, if desired, delete them.

If you need to keep the objects, you can try getting rid of the notice by informing Excel that it is OK for the objects to move. This involves a properties change for each of the objects—right-click the object and choose Properties, then check or clear the checkbox that controls whether the object can move.

5

Graphics as Watermarks

Watermarks in Excel

Excel does not have the ability to easily create and print watermarks. Granted, you can use the Background feature of Excel to add a graphic that appears "behind" your worksheet, but that graphic does not appear in Print Preview, will not print on the printer, and doesn't transfer to any Web page you make create from the spreadsheet. (See the Microsoft Knowledge Base, article 213977.)

This is amazing, particularly since people often use Excel to create and maintain confidential information and including a watermark that indicates confidentiality would be helpful. So how do you create a watermark to show that information is a draft or it is confidential? There are a couple of ways you can work around this deficiency.

First of all, some printers have the ability to produce watermarks and place them on your output. Check out your printer's documentation to see if your printer can do this. If it can, this is definitely the easiest solution.

You can create a watermark using WordArt and then manually place it on each output page, as desired. When creating the WordArt, format the colors to SemiTransparent and use a light gray fill for the art. This approach takes quite a bit of trial-and-error to get exactly what you want, and you must place the graphic on each page of your output.

Another workaround is that you can simply perform two printing passes. Create your watermark in Word and then print it on the page. Then run the paper through the printer again, this time printing from Excel. This may sound convoluted, but it is no more of a bother than any of the other workarounds. It also has the added benefit of a smaller Excel file since you aren't saving graphics with the file.

Printing a Draft Watermark

In Word, I can create a watermark that prints "behind" each page of my document. I have this nifty little technique that allows me to have the word "DRAFT" appear in light shading, behind the text of the document.

Excel is a different story. I can't get such a feature to work in Excel at all. It doesn't provide a means to create and print watermarks. Some people try to use the Background feature of Excel (Format | Sheet | Background) to create watermarks. This adds a graphic "behind" your worksheet, but that graphic does not appear in Print Preview, will not print on the printer, and doesn't transfer to any Web page you create from the spreadsheet. (See the Microsoft Knowledge Base, article 213977.)

The inability to create watermarks in Excel is amazing to many of us who have been using Excel for years. Instead, we have all been forced to scramble around for workarounds that will hopefully suffice until a better solution comes along.

One workaround is to use WordArt to create a watermark. You can manually place the graphic on each page, and it will print in the output. If you format the colors in the WordArt to SemiTransparent and use a light gray fill, then you may get just the look you want. There are drawbacks to this approach, of course, with the chief one being the inconvenience of engaging in the trial-and-error necessary to get the desired results.

For some people, their printers provide the solution. Some printers have the capability to create watermarks. For instance, the driver for the HP 5550 LaserJet allows you to do this. You can, in the Print dialog box, click on Properties to display what can be done with the printer, directly. Poke around on all the tabs and in all the controls, and you may find that your printer will create the watermark for you.

Other people use the approach of performing two printing passes. They do one pass in which the watermark is printed. Then, they feed the paper back through the printer to print the actual worksheet data.

Another approach is to create your watermark as a picture, using your favorite image editing software. Make sure the picture is large enough to cover a full sheet of paper, with the word "DRAFT" positioned diagonally in the center of the page. Then, in Excel, go to Page Setup and add the picture to the header. You can adjust its brightness or contrast to get the desired effect.

Finally, there are third-party solutions that you can use to put watermarks on the page for you. An example of this type of utility is FinePrint, which can be found at http://fineprint.com. (A quick search of the Internet should turn up other competing products you may want to consider, as well.)

Inserting a Watermark Behind Merged Cells

Tony asked if it was possible to insert a "watermark" type of permanent comment into a group of merged cells. The idea is for the comment to stay behind any entered text.

The short answer is that there is no way of doing this. Excel allows you to use a graphic as a background, but only for the worksheet as a whole, not for a range of cells. Even then, the background won't print—which is why Excel calls it a "background" and not a "watermark." (True watermarks are on physical paper, not on-screen.)

One possible solution—if you want your "comment" to be text instead of a graphic—is to use a text box. Create a text box that is the same size as your merged cells, and position it over those cells. Then, add your comment to the text box, as desired. Format the text box so the font is a light gray, the text box has no border, and the background is transparent.

The background being transparent is important, since you cannot position the text box "behind" the worksheet. The text box is on the drawing layer, which is always over the worksheet. You can arrange objects on the drawing layer, but you cannot move the drawing layer itself.

Now, if people use the Tab key to move into the merged cells, they can type things and it will appear in the cells. You may have to play with colors and appearance, because the gray text in the text box doesn't go away when you enter text in the underlying cells.

You should know that if someone uses the mouse to click on the merged cells, they will, instead, select the text box. You can get around this by selecting the merged cells, making sure they aren't protected, and then protecting the worksheet as a whole. By default, text boxes are protected, so they can't be selected in a protected worksheet. Now, when someone clicks on the merged cell, it is the cell that is selected, not the text box—it cannot be selected in a protected worksheet.

Non-Tiled Background Pictures

When you add a background picture to an Excel worksheet, the picture is normally "tiled" so that it fills the whole screen, over and over again. For some background images, this is a great effect. For others, it is bothersome. In these cases, you may want to have only a single copy of the background image appear on-screen.

There is no way to do this directly within Excel, however. The only option is the tiling of background images. You can reduce the bothersome effects of the tiling, though, by loading the background image into your favorite graphics editing program and simply increasing the size of the canvas on which the image is located. You should make the canvas the same size as a full sheet of paper, with the actual image centered on the canvas. Save the new image, and use it for your background.

6

Using Macros with Graphics

Positioning a Graphic in a Macro

Felix is writing a macro to add a graphic to a worksheet. He needs to position the graphic relative to the top-left corner of a particular cell. He wonders how he can place the graphic, within the macro code, so it is just to the right and beneath the upper-left corner of a given cell.

This task is relatively easy to do if you realize that each cell in a worksheet has both a Top and Left property that defines the location of both the top and left edges of the cell. You can adjust those values, slightly, to get the offset that you want, in this manner:

```
Dim rCell As Range
Set rCell = Range("A2")
With ActiveSheet.Shapes("Picture 1")
    .Top = rCell.Top + 5
    .Left = rCell.Left + 3
End With
```

Note that after this code is executed the graphic (defined by the name Picture 1) is placed just below the top edge of cell A2 and just to the right of its left edge.

Pasting a Graphic to Multiple Worksheets

Marty has a series of workbooks, some with as many as 50 worksheets. He needs to paste a graphic (a company logo) into the same spot on each worksheet. He tried to do this by selecting all the worksheets and then doing the pasting, but that didn't seem to work on multiple worksheets like regular editing does.

Marty is right; trying to paste a graphic when you have multiple worksheets selected doesn't work. When you try, Excel tells you that it cannot make the paste, but if you then select just a single worksheet you can paste quite nicely.

Instead, you need to use a macro to do the pasting. Assuming that the graphic has already been copied to the Clipboard, you can run a macro such as the following:

```
Sub InsertLogo1()
    Dim shtSheet As Worksheet

    Application.ScreenUpdating = False
    For Each shtSheet In Worksheets
        With shtSheet
            .Activate
            .Range("A1").Select
            .Paste
        End With
    Next
    Set shtSheet = Nothing
    Application.ScreenUpdating = True
End Sub
```

The macro steps through each worksheet in the workbook and pastes the graphic into cell A1. If you want to use a different cell, then all you need to do is modify the line that selects the cell.

If you don't want to copy the graphic to the Clipboard ahead of time, you can use a macro such as the following to insert the graphic directly from an image file:

```
Sub InsertLogo2()
    Dim strPath As String
    Dim shtSheet As Worksheet

    strPath = "C:\GraphicFolder\PictureName.bmp"

    For Each shtSheet In Worksheets
        shtSheet.Activate
        Range("A1").Select
        ActiveSheet.Pictures.Insert (strPath)
    Next shtSheet
    Set shtSheet = Nothing
End Sub
```

You can, of course, modify the path to the graphic file and the cell at which the file is pasted into the worksheets.

Assigning Macros to Graphics

You already know that Excel allows you to add graphics to your worksheets, such as pictures. You may not know, however, that you can assign macros to these graphics. With a macro associated with a graphic, the macro is executed whenever someone clicks on the graphic.

To assign a macro to a graphic, follow these steps:

1. Right-click on the graphic. Excel displays a Context menu.
2. Select the Assign Macro option from the Context menu. Excel displays the Assign Macro dialog box.

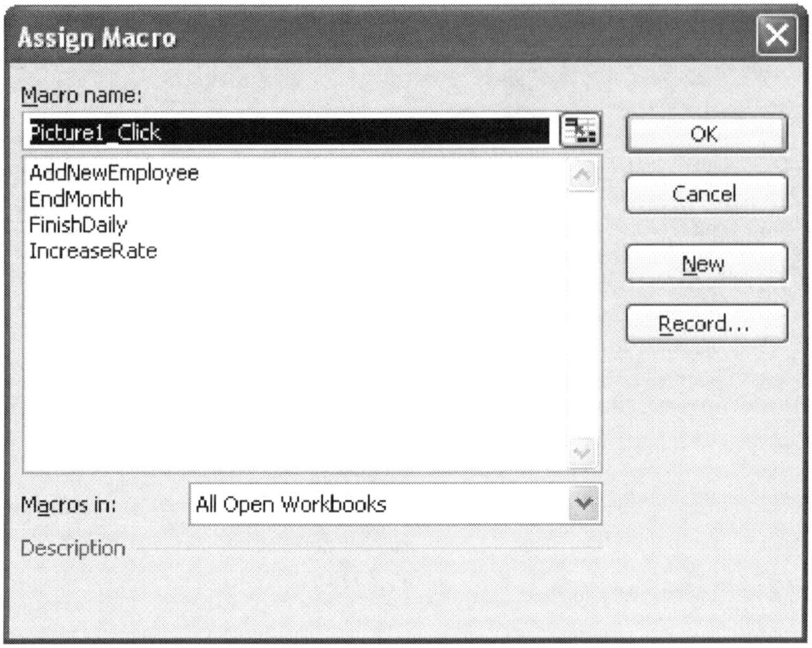

The Assign Macro dialog box.

3. Select the macro you want associated with the graphic.
4. Click on OK.

Save your workbook and test out your assignment by clicking on the graphic. The macro should run, as desired.

Unhiding or Listing All Objects

Mike had a problem where he knew that there were objects hidden within his workbook and he wanted to find them all. It seems he wrote a macro that hid some objects, but then did not unhide them.

If you want to simply find out the names of the objects in a worksheet, the following macro will do so very nicely. It shows not only the name, but also the type of object.

```
Sub ListObjects()
    Dim objCount As Integer
    Dim x As Integer
    Dim objList As String
    Dim objPlural As String
    Dim objType(17) As String

    'Set types for different objects
    objType(1) = "Autoshape"
    objType(2) = "Callout"
    objType(3) = "Chart"
    objType(4) = "Comment"
    objType(7) = "EmbeddedOLEObject"
    objType(8) = "FormControl"
    objType(5) = "Freeform"
    objType(6) = "Group"
    objType(9) = "Line"
    objType(10) = "LinkedOLEObject"
    objType(11) = "LinkedPicture"
    objType(12) = "OLEControlObject"
    objType(13) = "Picture"
    objType(14) = "Placeholder"
    objType(15) = "TextEffect"
    objType(17) = "TextBox"

    objList = ""

    'Get the number of objects
    objCount = ActiveSheet.Shapes.Count

    If objCount = 0 Then
        objList = "There are no shapes on " & _
          ActiveSheet.Name
    Else
        objPlural = IIf(objCount = 1, "", "s")
        objList = "There are " & Format(objCount, "0") _
          & " Shape" & objPlural & " on " & _
          ActiveSheet.Name & vbCrLf & vbCrLf
        For x = 1 To objCount
            objList = objList & ActiveSheet.Shapes(x).Name & _
              " is a " & objType(ActiveSheet.Shapes(x).Type) _
              & vbCrLf
        Next x
    End If

    MsgBox (objList)

End Sub
```

This macro returns the names and types of all objects in the worksheet. Another approach, however, is to display all the object names and then, if the object is hidden, ask if you want it unhidden. The following macro does just that:

```
Sub ShowEachShape1()
    Dim sObject As Shape
    Dim sMsg As String
    For Each sObject In ActiveSheet.Shapes
        sMsg = "Found " & IIf(sObject.Visible, _
          "visible", "hidden") & " object " & _
          vbNewLine & sObject.Name
        If sObject.Visible = False Then
            If MsgBox(sMsg & vbNewLine & "Unhide ?", _
              vbYesNo) = vbYes Then
                sObject.Visible = True
            End If
        Else
            MsgBox sMsg
        End If
    Next
End Sub
```

If you want the macro to only work on hidden objects and ignore those that are visible, then you can modify the macro to the following:

```
Sub ShowEachShape2()
    Dim sObject As Shape
    Dim sMsg As String
    For Each sObject In ActiveSheet.Shapes
        If sObject.Visible = False Then
            sMsg = "Object & sObject.Name & _
              " is hidden. Unhide it?"
            If MsgBox(sMsg, vbYesNo) = vbYes Then
                sObject.Visible = True
            End If
        End If
    Next
End Sub
```

To simply make all the objects visible in one step, you can shorten the macro even more:

```
Sub ShowEachShape3()
    Dim sObject As Shape
    For Each sObject In ActiveSheet.Shapes
        sObject.Visible = True
    Next
End Sub
```

Creating a Photo Catalog from a Folder of Photos

Glenn is making a catalog of all his digital photos in Excel. All the photos (about 5000 of them) are in a single folder. He would like to insert the photos to the right of the photo's description, then put a hyperlink to all the photos to enlarge the thumbnail to a larger photo. Right now Glenn is doing this one by one and it is driving him crazy, so he is looking for ways to speed the process up.

The good news is that you don't have to go crazy quite as fast; Excel provides macros that can make the job faster and easier. Before jumping into that discussion, however, you may want to think long and hard before you go about putting all your photos into an Excel workbook.

When you insert a photo into Excel, the file size of your workbook is increased by at least the file size of the photo being inserted. Thus, if your average photo is 1 MB in size (quite small with today's cameras) and you insert 5000 such photos, then you end up with a workbook that has at least 5 GB of photos in it. That is a huge workbook, and Excel might have a hard time working with that much info. (How hard of a time depends on your version of Excel, how much memory is in your system, how fast your processor is, etc.)

You might think that the solution is to scale the images as you place them in your worksheet, so that they are smaller. While rescaling an image makes it appear smaller (it looks smaller in the worksheet), it isn't really smaller. The full-size image is still right there in Excel. So, you don't reduce your workbook's file size at all by scaling the photos.

The way you can reduce the file size is to scale the photos outside of Excel, using photo editing software, before they are inserted into Excel. In other words, you would need to load each of the photos into the photo editing software, resize the photos to whatever thumbnail size you want, and then save the resized photo into a new thumbnail image file. (You generally wouldn't want to save the resized image over the top of your original photo.) You could then insert each thumbnail into your Excel worksheet and your resultant workbook file size would be smaller, although still directly related to the aggregate size of the thumbnail photos you add to the worksheet.

If you still want to insert all the photos into your worksheet, you can do so using a macro. The following example, PhotoCatalog, can look for all the thumbnail photos and insert them into the worksheet, along with a hyperlink to the full photo. It assumes four things: (1) your photos and thumbnails are all JPG images, (2) the photos are in the directory c:\Photos\, (3) the thumbnails are in the directory c:\Photos\Thumbnails\, and (4) the thumbnails have the same file names as the full-size photos.

```
Sub PhotoCatalog()
    Dim i As Double
    Dim xPhoto As String
    Dim sLocT As String
    Dim sLocP As String
    Dim sPattern As String

    sLocT = "c:\Photos\Thumbnails\"
    sLocP = "c:\Photos\"
    sPattern = sLocT & "*.jpg"

    Application.EnableEvents = False
    Application.ScreenUpdating = False

    Range("A1").Select
    ActiveCell.FormulaR1C1 = "Description"
    Range("B1").Select
    ActiveCell.FormulaR1C1 = "Thumbnail"
    Range("C1").Select
    ActiveCell.FormulaR1C1 = "Hyperlink"
    Range("A1:C1").Select
    With Selection.Font
        .Name = "Arial"
        .FontStyle = "Bold"
        .Size = 12
        .ColorIndex = xlAutomatic
    End With
    With Selection.Borders(xlEdgeBottom)
        .LineStyle = xlContinuous
        .Weight = xlMedium
        .ColorIndex = xlAutomatic
    End With

    i = 1
    On Error GoTo 0
    xPhoto = Dir(sPattern, vbNormal)
    Do While xPhoto <> ""
        i = i + 1
        Range("B" & i).Select
        ActiveSheet.Pictures.Insert(sLocT & xPhoto).Select
        With Selection.ShapeRange
            .LockAspectRatio = msoTrue
```

```
            .Height = 54#
            .PictureFormat.Brightness = 0.5
            .PictureFormat.Contrast = 0.5
            .PictureFormat.ColorType = msoPictureAutomatic
        End With
        Range("C" & i).Select
        ActiveSheet.Hyperlinks.Add Anchor:=Selection, _
          Address:= sLocP & xPhoto, TextToDisplay:=xPhoto
        xPhoto = Dir
    Loop

    Application.EnableEvents = True
    Application.ScreenUpdating = True
End Sub
```

It can take quite a while for this macro to run, depending on the type of system you are using and how many photos you are cataloging.

Removing Pictures for a Worksheet in VBA

Rob wrote about a problem he was having removing pictures from a worksheet. He has macros that add a picture (a signature) as a shape, but when he later tries to delete the picture, he cannot find it in the Shapes collection.

There are a couple of things to check out. First of all, you should ensure that you are using the proper syntax to do the deletion. Check to make sure you are explicitly including the sheet object in your code. For instance, the following line will not work:

```
Shapes(1).Delete
```

Instead, you must specify the sheet, using code similar to any of the following lines:

```
ActiveSheet.Shapes(1).Delete
Sheets("Sheet1").Shapes(1).Delete
Sheets(1).Shapes("Signature").Delete
```

If you determine that the expected image is not in the Shapes collection, then it is possible that Excel (for strange reasons only known to Excel) moved the image to a different collection, such as the Pictures collection. If you suspect this, then try using the following macro:

```
Sub WhatAmI()
    Dim sTemp As String

    sTemp = "You selected this type of object: " & TypeName(Selection)
    sTemp = sTemp & vbCrLf
    sTemp = sTemp & "It's name is " & Selection.Name
    MsgBox sTemp
End Sub
```

Select the signature image, then run the macro. You should see a message box that indicates the type of object you selected, along with its name. You can then use the information to modify your macro so it deletes the image, as desired.

Shifting Objects Off a Sheet

Mudit ran into problems when trying to delete rows and columns in a worksheet. He sometimes gets the message "Cannot shift object off this sheet." Other people report getting the message when they try to insert rows or column.

What is happening is that an object—such as a graph, drawing object, text box, picture, or even comment—cannot be correctly handled by Excel after the deletion or insertion. If the error occurs when inserting rows or columns, it means that the insertion would push the object beyond the right or bottom boundaries of the worksheet. The solution, of course, is to check whatever is at the right or bottom of the worksheet and make changes to those objects (move or delete them) as necessary.

If the error occurs while deleting rows or columns, it is normally because there are objects attached to cells within those rows or columns, and deleting the rows or columns would leave the objects "orphaned" in some way. For instance, let's say you are deleting column D, and there is an object associated with cell D4. The object doesn't need to be situation over column D; it could be several columns away, but still belong to cell D4. If you delete column D, then the object no longer has an anchor point. Excel's solution? Don't let column D be deleted until you do something with the object that would be orphaned by the edit.

The problem can also occur if the objects in a worksheet are formatted so that they cannot be moved or sized automatically by Excel, and then you try to delete columns or rows associated with the objects. In this case, you may want to try changing the formatting of the objects in the worksheet. If you have a lot of such objects in the worksheet, the following macro can be helpful in making the change:

```
Sub ResetShapes()
    Dim s As Shape
    On Error Resume Next
    For Each s In ActiveSheet.Shapes
        s.Placement = xlMoveAndSize
    Next
End Sub
```

Microsoft provides a Knowledge Base article that can be helpful with this problem. The article specifically addresses the issue of hiding rows and columns, but the solutions work when you are trying to delete them, as well. You can check it out at this page:

```
http://support.microsoft.com/?kbid=211769
```

If you are using Excel 97, you should reference this page, instead:

```
http://support.microsoft.com/?kbid=170081
```

Determining Mouse Cursor Coordinates On a Graphic

Gerald notes that when moving the mouse over a picture on a worksheet the mouse pointer is a cross. He wants to know how he can determine, using VBA, the coordinates of the cross when the mouse is clicked.

Excel doesn't allow you (even with VBA) to get the coordinates of the mouse pointer on a graphic inserted as a regular picture in the worksheet. If you insert the picture using an Image object in the Control toolbox, you have quite a bit more latitude. Indeed, you can use the MouseDown event handler to determine the coordinates, as shown here:

```
Private Sub Image1_MouseDown(ByVal Button As Integer, _
  ByVal Shift As Integer, ByVal X As Single, _
  ByVal Y As Single)
    MsgBox X & ", " & Y
End Sub
```

This code assumes that the image is named Image1. Similar code could be used to display the cursor coordinates in real time on the status bar:

```
Private Sub Image1_MouseMove(ByVal Button As Integer, _
  ByVal Shift As Integer, ByVal X As Single, _
  ByVal Y As Single)
    Application.StatusBar = Round(X, 0) & "," & Round(Y, 0)
End Sub
```

Either (or both) of these event handlers are obviously associated with Image1, so they need to be added to the code window for that object.

7

Creating AutoShapes

Creating a Drawing Object

Excel allows you to create drawing objects you can use in your worksheets. These objects (such as an oval, rectangle, line, or AutoShape) are positioned on what is termed the "drawing layer," which is separate and distinct from the values or formulas in the cells of your worksheet. You generally create such objects by using the tools on the Drawing toolbar. (Display the Drawing toolbar by clicking on the Drawing tool on the Standard toolbar.)

On the left side of the Drawing toolbar are several tools that are used to create basic shapes. The line, arrow, rectangle, and oval tools are easily identifiable. In addition, you can use the AutoShapes tool to display a menu of more than 125 different symbols, banners, and callouts. Follow these steps to place a drawing object in your worksheet:

1. Make sure the Drawing toolbar is displayed.
2. Click on the tool that represents the type of object you want to create. If you are creating an AutoShape, click on the AutoShape tool, then choose the shape from the appropriate submenu. Once a tool is selected, the mouse pointer changes to crosshairs, or a plus sign.
3. Click within your worksheet at one corner of where you want the shape to appear.
4. Drag the mouse to the opposite corner for the object.

5. When you release the mouse button, the object appears in the worksheet and you can manipulate it as desired.

Creating an AutoShape

In addition to working with numbers and text within cells of a workbook, Excel allows you to highlight your worksheets by adding simple drawings. One classification of drawing objects you can add are called ***AutoShapes.*** In many respects AutoShapes can be considered simple drawing objects because they are very simple to create, even though they appear complex. Excel defines quite a few different AutoShapes (over a hundred), all selectable by clicking on the AutoShapes tool on the Drawing toolbar.

When you click on the AutoShapes tool you actually display a series of menus from which you can pick the shape you want. For instance, let's say you wanted to draw a heart. You would click on the AutoShapes tool, then choose Basic Shapes, and finally choose the heart shape.

Once you select a shape, you draw it by positioning the mouse pointer at one corner of where you want to place the shape, clicking the mouse button, and dragging until you reach the opposite corner. When you release the mouse button the shape appears on the screen.

Adding AutoShapes

The graphics features of Excel allow you to add a number of predefined shapes to a workbook. These shapes, called AutoShapes, cover a wide range of needs. If you want to add shapes to the AutoShapes feature, however, you are out of luck. The shapes are apparently hard-coded into Excel and cannot be modified.

You can, however, add shapes to the Clip Gallery. If you format the shapes as WMF files, they are easy to add and easy to place within a worksheet. For instance, if you have a number of different flowchart symbols that you want to make available in Excel, all you need to do is save each symbol in the WMF format and then import them into the Clip Gallery. (To save graphics in the

WMF format, you will need to use a specialized graphics program, such as Paint Shop Pro or Corel Draw.)

If you don't want to use the Clip Gallery for some reason, you can simulate your own AutoShapes through a combination of macros and graphics in a hidden worksheet. The following general steps detail how to do this for a series of twenty flowchart symbols. The steps assume that you are reasonably comfortable writing macros and customizing toolbars.

1. Open a template workbook, and make sure it has only a single worksheet.
2. Place all the flowchart graphics on the worksheet.
3. Create a new toolbar, name it MyShapes, and make sure it is associated with the template workbook.
4. Add twenty buttons to the toolbar, one for each flowchart graphic. The idea is that clicking a button will add the associated flowchart shape to the active worksheet.
5. Edit each button face to show as closely as possible each flowchart graphic. (This is the toughest part of these steps.)
6. Change the ToolTip text for each button, as desired. This is helpful so the user can understand the purpose of each flowchart graphic.
7. In turn, select and name each of the flowchart graphics. (You name the graphics by selecting them and entering a name in the Name box at the left of the Formula bar.) For the purposes of these steps, assume you use names such as FlowObj1, FlowObj2, etc.
8. Write twenty macros (one for each flowchart graphic) of the following kind:

```
Sub AddFlowObj1()
    ThisWorkbook.Sheets(1).Shapes("FlowObj1").Copy
    ActiveSheet.Paste
End Sub
```

9. Assign each of the macros to the corresponding toolbar button.
10. In the Workbook module of the template, add the following procedures:

```
Private Sub Workbook_Open()
    Application.CommandBars("MyShapes").Visible = True
End Sub

Private Sub Workbook_BeforeClose(Cancel As Boolean)
    Application.CommandBars("MyShapes").Delete
End Sub
```

11. Save the template as an Excel add-in.
12. Restart Excel and use Tools | Add-ins to active your new add-in.

Displaying the AutoShapes Menu

If you have used Excel for any length of time, chances are pretty good that you are already familiar with AutoShapes and how to add them to your worksheets. If you have quite a few AutoShapes to insert in a document, you may find it handy to work with a floating AutoShapes menu instead of using the AutoShapes option on the Drawing toolbar. There are two ways you can display the floating AutoShapes menu. The first involves the use of the Drawing toolbar to get started:

1. Display the Drawing toolbar. (Click on the Drawing option on the Standard toolbar.)
2. Click on the AutoShapes option on the Drawing toolbar. The AutoShapes menu appears.
3. Position the mouse pointer over the bar at the top of the AutoShapes menu.
4. Click and drag the AutoShapes menu away from the Drawing toolbar.
5. Release the mouse button. You now have a floating AutoShapes menu.

The AutoShapes menu.

The other method of displaying the floating AutoShapes menu is even a bit simpler:

1. Choose Picture from the Insert menu. Excel displays a submenu.
2. Choose AutoShapes from the submenu. Excel displays both the Drawing toolbar and the floating AutoShapes menu.

Drawing Lines

Excel provides tools that allow you to create a number of shapes that were previously only available through the use of a drawing program. One of these shapes is a line. (Yes, the simple line!) Here's the easiest way to create your line:

1. Select a line weight and type by clicking on the Line Style tool on the toolbar.
2. Click on the line tool.
3. Position the mouse pointer where one end of the line is to be located.
4. Click and hold the mouse button.
5. Drag the mouse until the line is the desired length.
6. Release the mouse button.

Drawing Simple Objects

Excel includes a feature that allows you to add graphic objects to your worksheets. For the sake of this tip, ***simple objects*** include lines, arrows, rectangles (or squares), and ovals (or circles). These are considered simple because it only takes three quick steps to draw each of them.

Drawing objects that involve lines (such as lines and arrows) requires only that you perform a few steps:

1. Display the Drawing toolbar and select either the Line or Arrow tool by clicking on it with the mouse. (You may need to click the AutoShapes menu first.)
2. Move the mouse to the starting point for the line or arrow and click and hold the mouse button.

3. Move the mouse to the other end of the line and release the mouse button.

As you move the mouse in Step 2, notice that Excel displays a line that shows the approximate size, angle, and position of the line or arrow you are creating. When you release the mouse button (step 3), the line or arrow is redrawn in its final position and appearance. If you are drawing an arrow, the arrowhead appears at the end of the line where you ended your drawing (Step 3).

As with lines, the other simple objects only require two points to define them. Each of them, regardless of the final shape, is defined by a rectangle. (Yes, even ellipses and circles are defined by a rectangle—one that contains the entire shape.) You only need to do the following:

1. If you are using the Drawing toolbar, select the drawing tool by clicking on it with the mouse. (You may need to click the AutoShapes menu first.)
2. Move the mouse to one corner of the rectangle that will define the boundary of the shape, typically the upper-left corner, and click and hold the mouse button.
3. Drag the mouse to the opposite rectangle corner (the lower-right) and release the mouse button.

Notice that as you perform step 2, the shape appears on the screen and is dynamically sized as long as you continue to hold down the mouse button and move the mouse. When you release the button, the object is drawn in its final size and shape.

If you want to create a square or a circle, both of which are special forms of rectangles and ovals, Excel makes it easy. All you need to do is hold down the **SHIFT** key as you drag the mouse to the second point. Thus, you click the mouse, hold down **SHIFT** as you move the mouse pointer, and then release the mouse button.

Duplicating Drawing Objects

The objects you create using the Drawing toolbar are made up of two types of objects—text and graphics. Many times you will have a need to duplicate an object in your drawing. You do this by using the Clipboard. All you need to do is select the object (or objects) you wish to duplicate and then copy them to the Clipboard. This is easily done with the Copy command from the Edit menu, or by pressing **Ctrl+C**. Paste the objects back into your drawing and then move them to the desired position.

Quickly Duplicating Drawing Objects

You probably know that you can copy drawing objects using the familiar copy (**Ctrl+C**) and paste (**Ctrl+V**) commands. You may not know that there are other ways—quicker ways—that you can accomplish the same task.

The first method simply entails selecting the object and pressing **Ctrl+D**. That's it; the object is duplicated. In addition, if you hold down the shortcut key for a few seconds, the "autorepeat" feature of your keyboard will kick in and you can duplicate the object a zillion times in short order. Once duplicated, you can move the new objects where ever you need them in your worksheet.

If you prefer to use the mouse, you can duplicate objects by holding down the **Ctrl** key as you click and drag the object you want to duplicate. When you release the mouse button, the object is duplicated at the point where you released the button.

Another benefit of both of these approaches is that you don't need to use the Clipboard. That means you won't disturb anything you previously copied to the Clipboard. These techniques work equally well for ClipArt, WordArt, and AutoShapes, as well as text boxes.

Inserting Multiple Drawing Objects

There may be times when you want to insert multiple drawing objects (such as squares, rectangles, ovals, or circles) in your worksheet. Rather than click on the drawing tools on the Drawing toolbar before creating each object, Excel provides a nifty shortcut. All you need to do is double-click on the drawing tool you want to use.

For instance, you can double-click on the Rectangle tool if you want to draw rectangles or squares. Excel "locks" the tool into place, and you can create as many of the objects as you desire. When you are done creating them, click on the tool again or press the **Esc** key to return the mouse pointer to normal.

You can apply the same concept to creating AutoShapes, but the process is just a bit longer. Follow these steps:

1. Click on the AutoShapes tool on the Drawing toolbar. Excel presents a listing of AutoShape categories.
2. Click on the category you want to use. Excel displays a wide array of AutoShapes you can use.
3. Notice that at the top of the AutoShapes menu there is a small horizontal bar. Click on this bar and drag it to some other location on your screen. When you release the mouse button, the AutoShapes menu appears on its own, floating on your desktop.
4. Double-click on any item on the menu. It remains selected.
5. Create any number of that AutoShape in your worksheet.
6. Press **Esc** or click on the AutoShape again (in the floating menu) to return the mouse pointer to normal.

8

Formatting AutoShapes

Changing an AutoShape

If you are using Excel's predefined shapes in your workbooks, there may be times when you want to completely change a shape from one to another. For instance, you may want to change one banner shape to another. While you can simply delete your original shape and then draw a new one, you can change an existing shape by following these steps:

1. Make sure the Drawing toolbar is displayed.
2. Select the AutoShape you want to change. Handles should appear around the outside of the shape.
3. Click your mouse on Draw on the Drawing toolbar, and then choose Change AutoShape. The familiar AutoShape categories appear.
4. Select the AutoShape you want to use.

Excel changes the shape used, without changing the overall size of the bounding rectangle that contains the shape. You can then proceed to edit the new shape, as desired.

Rotating a Drawing Object

Excel allows you to create drawing objects in your worksheets. These objects (such as an oval, rectangle, line, or AutoShape) are positioned on what is termed the "drawing layer," which is separate and distinct from the contents of the worksheet. You generally create such objects by using the tools on the Drawing toolbar.

You can rotate the drawing object to any degree you desire. Simply follow these steps:

1. Select the drawing object.
2. If you are using Excel 97 or Excel 2000, click on the Free Rotate tool on the Drawing toolbar. Green rotation handles appear at the corners of the drawing object. (In later versions of Excel there is no Free Rotate tool on the Drawing toolbar. Instead, a single green rotation handle appears by the object whenever you select it.)

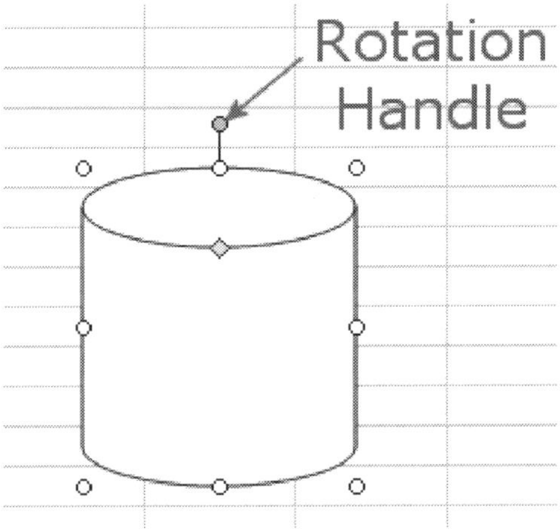

Rotation handle.

3. Click on a rotation handle and drag the object in the direction desired.
4. Press **Esc** when you are done rotating the object.

If you know exactly how much you want to rotate the drawing object, you can also do the following:

1. Right-click on the drawing object. Excel displays a Context menu.
2. Choose the Format AutoShape option from the Context menu. This displays the Format AutoShape dialog box.
3. Make sure the Size tab is selected.

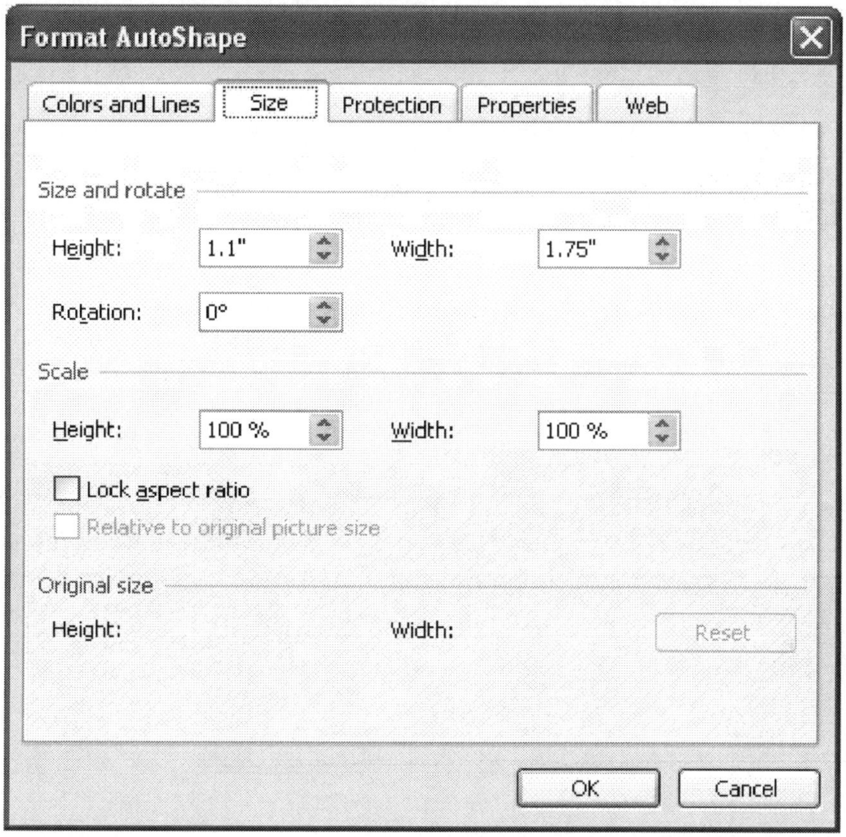

The Size tab of the Format AutoShape dialog box.

4. Change the value in the Rotation box as desired.
5. Click on OK.

Flipping a Drawing Object

Once you have created a drawing object in Excel using the Drawing toolbar, you can flip it horizontally or vertically. To flip an object, follow these steps:

1. Select the pointer tool (the arrow) from the Drawing toolbar.
2. Using the mouse, point to the object you want to flip, then click on it. Excel places small square boxes (handles) around the object.
3. Choose the Rotate or Flip option from the Draw menu on the Drawing toolbar. Excel displays a submenu of available actions.
4. Click on either Flip Horizontal or Flip Vertical. Excel flips the object in the direction specified.

Changing the Size of a Drawing Object

You already know that you can use the Drawing toolbar to add graphic objects to your Excel worksheet. As you create and refine your drawings, there will doubtless be times when you need to change the size of objects. You can change the size of most objects by following these steps:

1. Select the Pointer tool from the Drawing toolbar.
2. Point to the object whose size you want to change, and then select it by clicking the mouse button. Excel displays small boxes called ***handles*** around the object.
3. Point to one of the handles, click on it, and hold down the mouse button.
4. Drag the mouse. The size of the object will change as you move the mouse.
5. Release the mouse button when the object is the desired size.

Filling a Drawing Object

When you first insert a drawing object in Excel, it appears as an outline; sort of a stick drawing. You may want to change this by filling the object with either a color or a specific effect. Both of these are done using the Fill tool on the Drawing toolbar. (This is the one that looks like a bucket spilling paint.) To use the tool, simply click on it using the mouse and then click on the object you want filled. It is then filled using the color shown in the bar at the bottom of the Fill tool.

If you want to change the color used for fills, you can do so by clicking on the down-arrow at the right of the Fill tool. This displays a palette of colors (forty of them) from which you can choose a color. If you don't like those colors, you can click on More Fill Colors (just underneath the palette) to pick any color you desire.

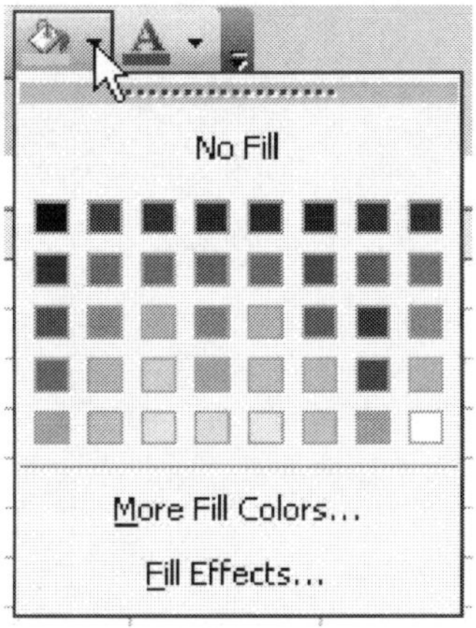

The color palette.

A neat feature of Excel is that you can also pick an effect to use for your fill. You do this by choosing Fill Effects at the bottom of the color palette. This displays the Fill Effects dialog box. Using the controls in this dialog box (and on the other tabs in the dialog box), you can specify exactly what special effects you want applied to filling the shape. You can choose to use a gradient (where the fill blends in, from none to full) or apply a texture (such as wood or marble). You can also use any of a number of different patterns, or use your own picture for the fill. The different fill options allow you to make your graphics look quite impressive.

Understanding Fill Effects

Excel is not a specialized graphics program, by any stretch of the imagination—it is a spreadsheet program. However, you can insert drawing objects which may be beneficial to the information you are trying to convey in the worksheet. You can apply a few fancy effects to your drawing objects when you fill them with a color. To see the available effects, follow these steps:

1. Select the drawing object you want to modify.
2. Click on the down-arrow next to the Fill Color tool on the Drawing toolbar. Excel displays a color menu.
3. From the color menu, click on Fill Effects. Excel displays the Fill Effects dialog box.

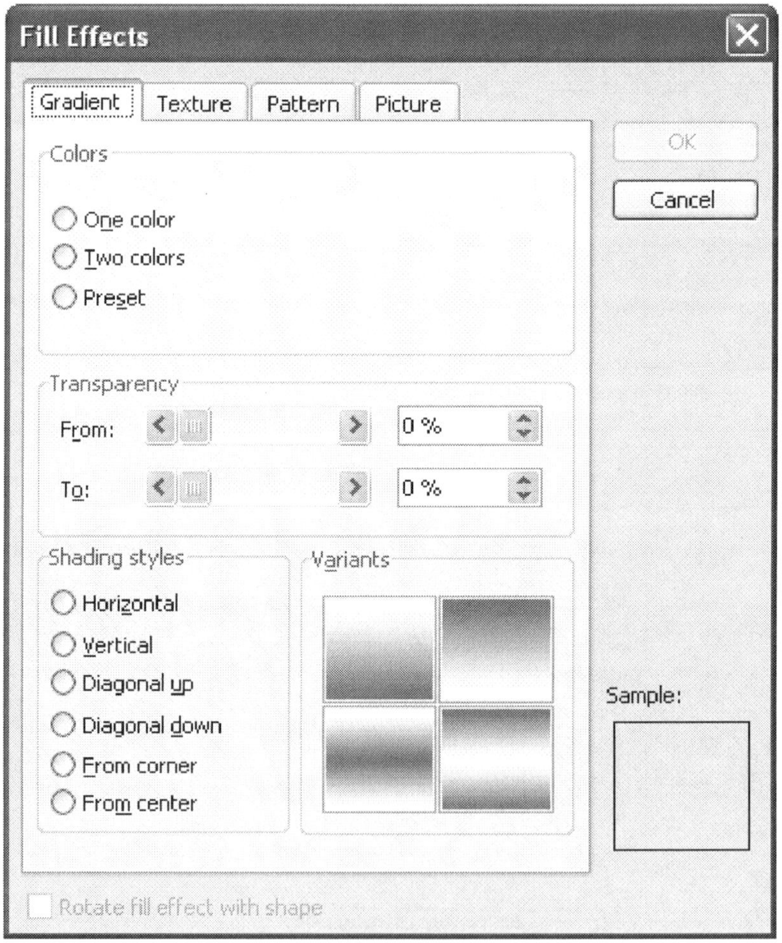

The Fill Effects dialog box.

You can use the tools in the dialog box to change how the filling in the drawing object is rendered. The tabs in the dialog box allow the following:

- **Gradient.** This tab is used to modify the density of the color used in various parts of the drawing object. You should experiment with these to get the desired effect.
- **Texture.** This tab displays many different surface textures you can use to fill your drawing object. There are some great marble, fabric, and wood textures provided with Excel.
- **Pattern.** This tab presents many different patterns you can use in conjunction with whatever fill color you have used. Many of the patterns are reminiscent of the patterns you can use in designing your Windows desktop.
- **Picture.** This tab allows you to pick a picture that is used to fill your drawing object. Depending on the picture you use, this can create some very interesting special effects.

Changing How Arrows Look

The Drawing toolbar in Excel allows you to place arrows within your workbook. Once an arrow is placed where you want it, you can easily change the way the arrow looks by following these steps:

1. Select the arrow by clicking on it. (You can tell if the arrow is selected by whether there are handles at each end of the arrow line.)
2. Choose AutoShape from the Format menu. Excel displays the Format AutoShape dialog box.
3. Make sure the Colors and Lines tab is selected.

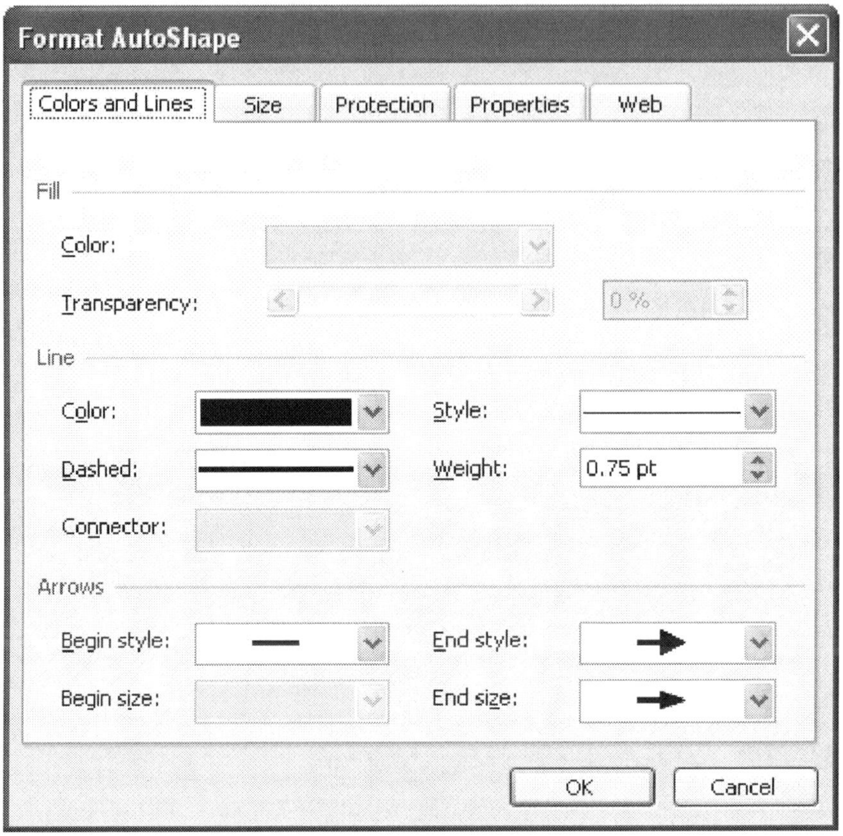

The Colors and Lines tab of the Format AutoShape dialog box.

4. Use the Begin Style and End Style drop-down lists to specify how each end of your arrow line should appear.
5. Use the Begin Size and End Size drop-down lists to specify the size of each arrowhead. (These drop-down lists are available only if you specified an actual arrowhead in the Begin Style and End Style drop-down lists.)
6. Click on OK. Your arrow is updated, as you specified.

Styles for Lines, Dashes, and Arrows

Excel allows you to place many different types of graphics objects within your worksheets. One common type of graphic object is a line or arrow. When you first insert lines or arrows into your worksheet, Excel places them using a thin line. You may want to change the width of the line used, as well as the style of line or arrow. Excel allows you to do this using three tools on the Drawing toolbar.

- The Line Style tool allows you to select a line width and style.
- The Dash Style tool is used to specify a non-solid style for the line
- The Arrow Style tool is used to indicate how you want the arrowheads to appear.

To use the tools, make sure you select the line you want changed before you click on a tool. You can change the line styles for any drawing composed of lines, but not for AutoShapes, rectangles, or ovals.

Setting Default Attributes for Lines and Arrows

Glenn adds lines and arrows regularly to flowcharts that he creates in Excel. He is wondering if there is a way to set a default line weight, color, and arrowhead, as it gets tedious to change the attributes all the time.

Setting defaults for AutoShapes (such as lines and arrows) is quite easy in Excel. Just follow these steps:

1. Draw your line or arrow as you normally would.
2. Format the line or arrow so that it appears just as you want it to.
3. Right-click on the line or arrow. Excel displays a Context menu.
4. From the Context menu select the option that sets the shape settings as default. Depending on your version of Excel, this option will be named something like Set AutoShape Defaults or Set Default Line.

That's it. For the rest of your current Excel session your lines and arrows will be drawn using your desired formats.

Changing Line Color in a Drawing Object

Lines are used for all graphics within Excel. Lines are typically used to outline the shape, although you can use them for arrows and for drawing directly on your worksheet. Excel allows you to specify the color or pattern that should be used for your lines. To change the line color used in an object, follow these steps:

1. Make sure the Drawing toolbar is displayed.
2. Click once on the object whose line color you want to change. The object is selected.
3. Click on the Line Color tool on the Drawing toolbar. The color of the lines in the object are changed to the color used in the bar at the bottom of the Line Color tool.
4. To use a different color, click on the down-arrow to the right of the tool and choose a different color.

Pictures in AutoShapes

Excel allows you to format the appearance of the AutoShapes you place in a worksheet. If you display the Format AutoShape dialog box, you can change all sorts of colors, lines, fills, fonts, and other attributes of the AutoShape. One really nifty formatting feature is to place a picture within an AutoShape. Follow these steps:

1. Create your AutoShape as you normally would.
2. Right-click the AutoShape. Excel displays a Context menu for the AutoShape.
3. Choose Format AutoShape from the Context menu. Excel displays the Format AutoShape dialog box. (If Format AutoShape was not one of the options from the Context menu, then you didn't right-click the

AutoShape itself in step 2. Make sure that you right-click one of the lines that make up the AutoShape.)

4. Display the Colors and Lines tab.

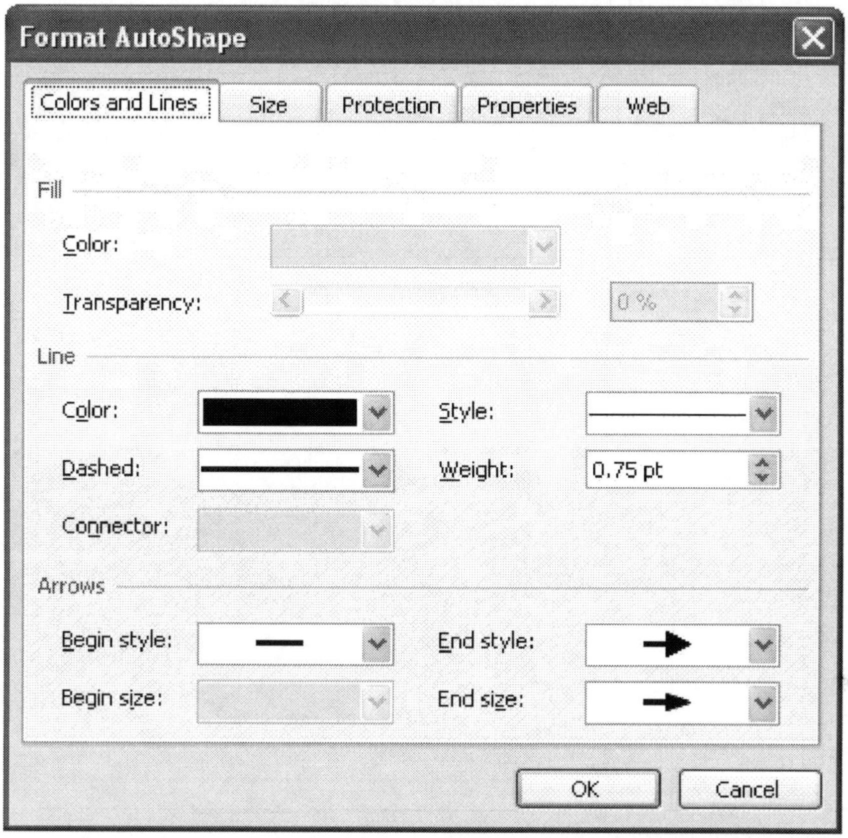

The Colors and Lines tab of the Format AutoShape dialog box.

5. Click the drop-down arrow for the Color drop-down list.
6. On the drop-down list, choose Fill Effects. Excel displays the Fill Effects dialog box.
7. Make sure the Picture tab is displayed.

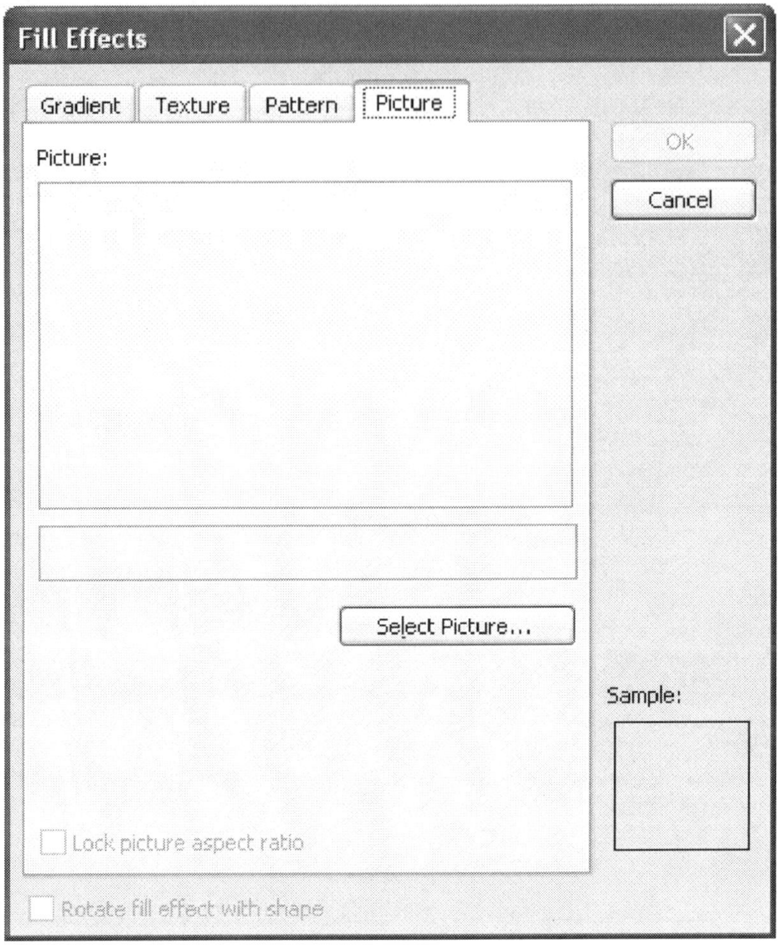

The Picture tab of the Fill Effects dialog box.

8. Use the controls in the dialog box to select a picture you want in the AutoShape.
9. Click OK as many times as necessary to close all the dialog boxes.

The picture you selected in step 8 should now appear in the background of the AutoShape. In most cases the AutoShape looks like a "mask" over the picture, which is a nice effect. You should also use this technique sparingly, as each picture you place in an AutoShape can greatly increase the size of your workbook.

Adding Text to an AutoShape

Most people know that you can add text boxes to your worksheet, but don't realize that you can actually add text to any AutoShape. Just follow these steps:

1. Add your AutoShape as you normally would.
2. Right-click the new AutoShape. Excel displays a Context menu.
3. Choose Add Text from the Context menu. An insertion point appears within the body of the AutoShape.
4. Type your desired text.
5. Click somewhere outside the boundaries of the AutoShape, such as within a cell of the worksheet.

If you later resize your AutoShape, then the text within it is reformatted to fit the new dimensions of the shape. (This behavior is the same that occurs if you resize a text box that contains text.)

Pulling AutoShape Text from a Worksheet Cell

AutoShapes are a great way to easily add simple graphics to your worksheets. Better still, AutoShapes are like text boxes, in that they can contain text.

If you know how to add text to a text box, you already know how to add text to an AutoShape. What you may not know how to do is to make that text dynamic, so that it is based on the text stored in a cell of your worksheet. Follow these steps:

1. Select the AutoShape that you want to contain the text. When it is selected (by clicking it once with the mouse), you'll see small selection handles around the exterior of the AutoShape.
2. Click once in the Formula bar.
3. Type an equal sign, and then click on the cell that contains the text you want in the AutoShape.
4. Press **ENTER**.

That's it; the text in the AutoShape is now tied to the text of the cell you specified in step 3. If you change that text, then the text in the AutoShape changes, as well.

Rounded Corners on Cells

Kartik wonders how he can get rounded borders on cells in Excel. The short answer is that you cannot; Excel allows you to place square-cornered borders, but not rounded-corner borders.

The only possible workaround is to create a drawing object that is a rectangle with rounded corners. If you make the drawing object the same size as your cells and format it so it has no fill color, you could copy the object to as many cells as you want to have the border. Remember, however, that this is just a workaround—if you change the size of the cell in which one of these drawing objects is located, the "border" won't resize with the cell; it will remain small.

9

Using Text Boxes

Using Text Boxes

A ***text box*** is a special kind of graphics object that is nothing but a box that can contain text. You can place any text in them you desire, using the same techniques you use to add text to a cell. The way in which you add a text box depends on the version of Excel you are using.

You create a text box in the following manner:

1. Make sure the Drawing toolbar is displayed. (You can display it by clicking on the Drawing tool on the Standard toolbar, or by choosing View | Toolbars | Drawing.)
2. Click on the Text Box tool on the Drawing toolbar. The mouse cursor becomes a small plus sign.
3. Click at a corner of where you want the text box to appear and, while holding down the mouse button, drag to the opposite corner.
4. Release the mouse button.
5. Start typing the text you want in the text box.

Once you create the text box and start typing, the text box remains selected. When you want to work with other parts of your worksheet, simply use the mouse to select those parts.

Sizing Text Boxes and Cells the Same

You already know that Excel allows you to create text boxes within your worksheets. You may have a need, at some point, to create a text box that is exactly the same size as a particular cell. If you only have one or two such text boxes to create, the easiest way is to follow these steps:

1. Display the Drawing toolbar.
2. Click on the Text Box tool.
3. Hold down the **Alt** key as you click and drag to create your text box.

When you hold down the **Alt** key, it forces Excel to "snap" the sides of your text box to a drawing grid which just happens to match the cell boundaries in your worksheet. The result is a text box that is exactly the desired size.

If you need to create quite a few of these text boxes, all at one time, you can turn the snap-to-gird feature on permanently. All you need to do is choose Draw (on the Drawing toolbar) | Snap | To Grid.

If you have many, many such text boxes to create, on lots of different workbooks, you can create the desired text boxes using a macro. The following macro will create a text box directly over the selected cell, and size it to be exactly the same size as the selected cell:

```
Sub TextBox2Cell()
    With ActiveCell
        ActiveSheet.Shapes.AddTextbox _
          msoTextOrientationHorizontal, .Left, _
          .Top, .Width, .Height
    End With
End Sub
```

With a small change in the macro, you can modify it so that it will create text boxes that are just as large as whatever range of cells you have selected:

```
Sub TextBox2Selection()
    If TypeName(Selection) = "Range" Then
        With Selection
            ActiveSheet.Shapes.AddTextbox _
              msoTextOrientationHorizontal, .Left, _
              .Top, .Width, .Height
        End With
```

```
    End If
End Sub
```

Regardless of which approach you use to create the text box (manual or macro), it should be noted that if you resize the cell by changing the column width or row height, the size of the text box will also change to match the new cell size.

Adding a Drop Shadow to a Text Box

Text boxes are a graphic element you can use in your workbooks to hold information that is ancillary to the main data in the workbook. For instance, you might use a text box to create a sidebar or other text object. To enhance your layout design using text boxes, you can add a drop shadow so the text box appears to float about the actual printed page.

To add a drop shadow to a text box, follow these steps:

1. Make sure the Drawing toolbar is displayed. (You can click on the Drawing tool on the Standard toolbar to display the Drawing toolbar.)
2. Select the text box you want to format. Small selection handles should appear around the perimeter of the text box.
3. Click on the Shadow tool on the Drawing toolbar. Excel displays a palette of available shadows.
4. Click on the shadow desired.

Counting All Characters

When you work with worksheets—particularly those from other people—you may be looking for a way count the number of characters in a worksheet. The following macro is very handy in that regard. It counts the number of characters in an entire workbook, including any characters in any text boxes inserted in the various worksheets.

```
Option Explicit
Sub CountCharacters()
    Dim wks As Worksheet
    Dim rng As Range
```

```
Dim rCell As Range
Dim shp As Shape

Dim bPossibleError As Boolean
Dim bSkipMe As Boolean

Dim lTotal As Long
Dim lTotal2 As Long
Dim lConstants As Long
Dim lFormulas As Long
Dim lFormulaValues As Long
Dim lTxtBox As Long
Dim sMsg As String

On Error GoTo ErrHandler
Application.ScreenUpdating = False

lTotal = 0
lTotal2 = 0
lConstants = 0
lFormulas = 0
lFormulaValues = 0
lTxtBox = 0
bPossibleError = False
bSkipMe = False
sMsg = ""

For Each wks In ActiveWorkbook.Worksheets
    ' Count characters in text boxes
    For Each shp In wks.Shapes
        If TypeName(shp) <> "GroupObject" Then
            lTxtBox = lTxtBox + shp.TextFrame.Characters.Count
        End If
    Next shp

    ' Count characters in cells containing constants
    bPossibleError = True
    Set rng = wks.UsedRange.SpecialCells(xlCellTypeConstants)
    If bSkipMe Then
        bSkipMe = False
    Else
        For Each rCell In rng
            lConstants = lConstants + Len(rCell.Value)
        Next rCell
    End If

    ' Count characters in cells containing formulas
    bPossibleError = True
    Set rng = wks.UsedRange.SpecialCells(xlCellTypeFormulas)
    If bSkipMe Then
        bSkipMe = False
    Else
```

```
            For Each rCell In rng
                lFormulaValues = lFormulaValues + Len(rCell.Value)
                lFormulas = lFormulas + Len(rCell.Formula)
            Next rCell
        End If
    Next wks

    sMsg = Format(lTxtBox, "#,##0") & _
      " Characters in text boxes" & vbCrLf
    sMsg = sMsg & Format(lConstants, "#,##0") & _
      " Characters in constants" & vbCrLf & vbCrLf

    lTotal = lTxtBox + lConstants

    sMsg = sMsg & Format(lTotal, "#,##0") & _
      " Total characters (as constants)" & vbCrLf & vbCrLf

    sMsg = sMsg & Format(lFormulaValues, "#,##0") & _
      " Characters in formulas (as values)" & vbCrLf
    sMsg = sMsg & Format(lFormulas, "#,##0") & _
      " Characters in formulas (as formulas)" & vbCrLf & vbCrLf

    lTotal2 = lTotal + lFormulas
    lTotal = lTotal + lFormulaValues

    sMsg = sMsg & Format(lTotal, "#,##0") & _
      " Total characters (with formulas as values)" & vbCrLf
    sMsg = sMsg & Format(lTotal2, "#,##0") & _
      " Total characters (with formulas as formulas)"

    MsgBox Prompt:=sMsg, Title:="Character count"

ExitHandler:
    Application.ScreenUpdating = True
    Exit Sub

ErrHandler:
    If bPossibleError And Err.Number = 1004 Then
        bPossibleError = False
        bSkipMe = True
        Resume Next
    Else
        MsgBox Err.Number & ": " & Err.Description
        Resume ExitHandler
    End If
End Sub
```

The macro may seem quite long, but it is very well structured in exactly what it does. First, it looks through all the text boxes in a worksheet. If they are not grouped (you cannot count characters in grouped text boxes), then the characters in them are tallied up. Then the macro tallies up the characters in cells containing constants. Finally, it counts all the characters used in cells containing formulas. The balance of the macro is used to present the information in a message box.

Finding and Replacing in Text Boxes

David wonders if it is possible to use Find and Replace to locate and modify text in text boxes or in labels in charts. The short answer is that it is not possible, but there are several workarounds you can try.

First, you could easily make the text in your text boxes or in your chart labels dynamic, so that it is tied to the contents of some worksheet cells. For instance, you could do the following for your text boxes:

1. Copy your text from each of text boxes to a range of cells on your worksheet. (For this example, assume that you copied the contents of ten text boxes to the range Z1:Z10.)
2. Select the first text box (the one that corresponds to cell Z1) and get rid of the text box's contents.
3. With the text box still selected, enter the following into the Formula bar: **=Z1**. When you press **ENTER**, the text box should reflect whatever is in cell Z1.
4. Repeat steps 2 and 3 for each of your other text boxes, using the appropriate cell reference for each in step 3.

That's it. You can use the same technique with custom chart labels—all you need to do is select the chart label and enter a cell reference in the Formula bar. With the text boxes and chart labels tied to worksheet cells, you can easily use Find and Replace to search for and change information in the cells. When the changes are made, the text boxes and chart labels should automatically reflect the changes in the cells.

The only way to actually change the text within a text box or chart label is to change it manually or change it using a macro. The code would need to step through each text box in the worksheet and then make your change. The following is a simple version of a macro that can make such a change.

```
Sub TextBoxReplace()
    Dim shp As Shape
    Dim sOld As String
    Dim sNew As String

    'Change as desired
    sOld = "Old string"
    sNew = "New string"
    On Error Resume Next
    For Each shp In ActiveSheet.Shapes
        With shp.TextFrame.Characters
            .Text = Application.WorksheetFunction.Substitute( _
              .Text, sOld, sNew)
        End With
    Next
End Sub
```

This macro steps through all the shapes in the worksheet (text boxes are shapes) and then replaces whatever is in the sOld variable with whatever is in the sNew variable. Applying the same technique to chart labels is only a bit more complex, as shown in the following macro:

```
Sub ChartLabelReplace()
    Dim Cht As ChartObject
    Dim Ser As Series
    Dim scPt As Point
    Dim sOld As String
    Dim sNew As String

    'Change as desired
    sOld = "Old String"
    sNew = "New String"
    On Error Resume Next
    For Each Cht In ActiveSheet.ChartObjects
        For Each Ser In Cht.Chart.SeriesCollection
            For Each scPt In Ser.Points
                With scPt.DataLabel
                    .Text = Application.WorksheetFunction.Substitute( _
                      .Text, sOld, sNew)
                End With
            Next
        Next
    Next
End Sub
```

The macro steps through each data label for every data series on every chart and (again) replaces any instances of whatever is in sOld with whatever is in sNew.

Resizing a Text Box in a Macro

Rob has a text box, in a worksheet, that contains text copied from Word. He wants to know how he can resize the text box using a macro, so that it covers a specific range of cells.

There are a couple of ways you can approach this task. One is to specify, in the macro, exactly which cells you want to cover with the text box, and then adjust the properties of the text box to match the characteristics of the cells you specify.

```
Sub ResizeBox1()
    Dim sTL As String
    Dim sBR As String
    Dim rng As Range

    ' Change top-left and bottom-right addresses as desired
    sTL = "A1"
    sBR = "M40"

    ' Ensure a text box is selected
    If TypeName(Selection) <> "TextBox" Then
        MsgBox "Text box not selected"
        Exit Sub
    End If

    With Selection
        Set rng = ActiveSheet.Range(sTL)
        .Top = rng.Top
        .Left = rng.Left
        Set rng = ActiveSheet.Range(sBR)
        .Width = rng.Left + rng.Width
        .Height = rng.Top + rng.Height
    End With
    Set rng = Nothing
End Sub
```

In order to use the macro, change the address of the cells you want to use for the top-left and bottom-right of the text box. Then, select the text box and run the macro.

If you prefer, you could use a named range to specify the range to be covered by the text box. The following macro expects that the range will be named RangeToCover. When you select the text box and run the macro, the text box is resized to match the size of the range.

```
Sub ResizeBox2()
    Dim l_rRangeToCover As Range
    Dim l_rLowerRight As Range

    ' Ensure a text box is selected
    If TypeName(Selection) <> "TextBox" Then
        MsgBox "Text box not selected"
        Exit Sub
    End If

    ' Get the range to cover
    Set l_rRangeToCover = _
      ActiveSheet.Range(Names("RangeToCover").RefersToRange.Value)

    ' Get its lower right cell
    Set l_rLowerRight = _
      l_rRangeToCover.Cells( _
      l_rRangeToCover.Rows.Count, _
      l_rRangeToCover.Columns.Count)

    ' Resize the text box
    With Selection
        .Left = l_rRangeToCover.Left
        .Top = l_rRangeToCover.Top
        .Width = l_rLowerRight.Left + l_rLowerRight.Width - .Left
        .Height = l_rLowerRight.Top + l_rLowerRight.Height - .Top
    End With
End Sub
```

Placing Text Box Text Into a Worksheet

Excel allows you to place all sorts of graphic objects on your worksheet. One type of graphic object actually contains text—a text box. If you have quite a few text boxes in a worksheet, you may be wondering if there is a way to extract the text from each text box and place it in the worksheet itself.

There is no command to do this; you must instead use a macro. The following macro steps through each text box in a worksheet and makes the desired extraction:

```
Sub ExtractText()
    Dim shp As Shape
    Dim sLoc As String

    For Each shp In ActiveSheet.Shapes
        With shp
            If Left(.Name, 8) = "Text Box" Then
                sLoc = .TopLeftCell.Address
                Do Until Range(sLoc) = ""
                    sLoc = Range(sLoc).Offset(1, 0).Address
                Loop
                Range(sLoc) =.TextFrame.Characters.Text
                .Delete
            End If
        End With
    Next
End Sub
```

Since Excel stores all graphic shapes in the Shapes collection, you can step through the collection and make a determination as to which shapes you want to work with. In this case, the first eight characters of the shape's name is checked. Only if the name begins with "Text Box" does the macro consider the shape to be a text box from which text can be extracted.

Rather than check for the "Text Box" wording in the name, the macro could also check to see what type of shape is being considered. If you prefer to do this, then simply replace the test line (If Left…) with the following test line:

```
            If shp.Type = msoTextBox Then
```

The sLoc variable is used to store the location of the text box, which is contained in the .TopLeftCell property. A Do loop is then used to make sure that the cell pointed to by the address is empty. (This prevents any existing contents of the cell from being overwritten.) If it is not empty, then the address is "incremented" to the next cell in the column.

With the address of an empty cell determined, the text of the text box is stored in the cell. The .Delete method is then used to get rid of the actual text box.

Adding Text Boxes to Charts

When you create a chart from your Excel data, you may want to add text boxes to the chart for any number of purposes (copyright statement, explanation, notes, etc.). There are two quick ways you can add a text box.

The first method is to use the Drawing toolbar. Simply make sure it is displayed, then click the Text Box tool. The mouse pointer changes to crosshairs, and you can click and drag to outline the text box you want created.

The second way to create a text box is to use the Formula bar. Make sure you select any part of your chart except a title or data label. Click in the Formula bar and start typing what you want to appear in the text box. When you press **ENTER**, the text you typed is placed in a text box in the center of the chart. You can then move and resize the text box, as desired.

10

Special Tools: WordArt and the Camera

Using WordArt in Excel

WordArt is a program that allows you to treat text as a graphic. You can use the program to add special effects and flourishes to text, and then insert the text—as a graphic—in your worksheet. It is useful for creating special text elements such as logos, mastheads, or titles. Don't confuse the program name (WordArt) with Microsoft Word; these are two entirely different programs, and you can use WordArt with Excel as easily as you can use it with Word.

How you access WordArt depends on the version of Excel you are using. Excel 97 includes WordArt 2.0, although it is not automatically installed when you install Word. You can tell if WordArt is installed by trying to access WordArt. If it is not installed, then you can run the Excel Setup program again and install WordArt on your system.

You access WordArt using either of these methods in Excel 97:

- Double-click on a graphic originally created with WordArt.
- Choose Object from the Insert menu. You will see the Object dialog box. Choose Microsoft WordArt 2.0 from the Object Type list and click on OK. You will see the WordArt dialog box.

When WordArt if running, you see the WordArt dialog box, and most of your Excel 97 menus and toolbars are hidden. When you are through using WordArt, you can exit the program simply by using the mouse to click somewhere else in your worksheet. (You can also press **Esc** to exit WordArt.)

Excel 2000 through Excel 2003 include a more integrated approach to WordArt. If you are using Excel 2000, Excel 2002, or Excel 2003 you should follow these steps:

1. Make sure the Drawing toolbar is displayed.
2. On the Drawing toolbar, click on the Insert WordArt tool. You then see the WordArt Gallery.

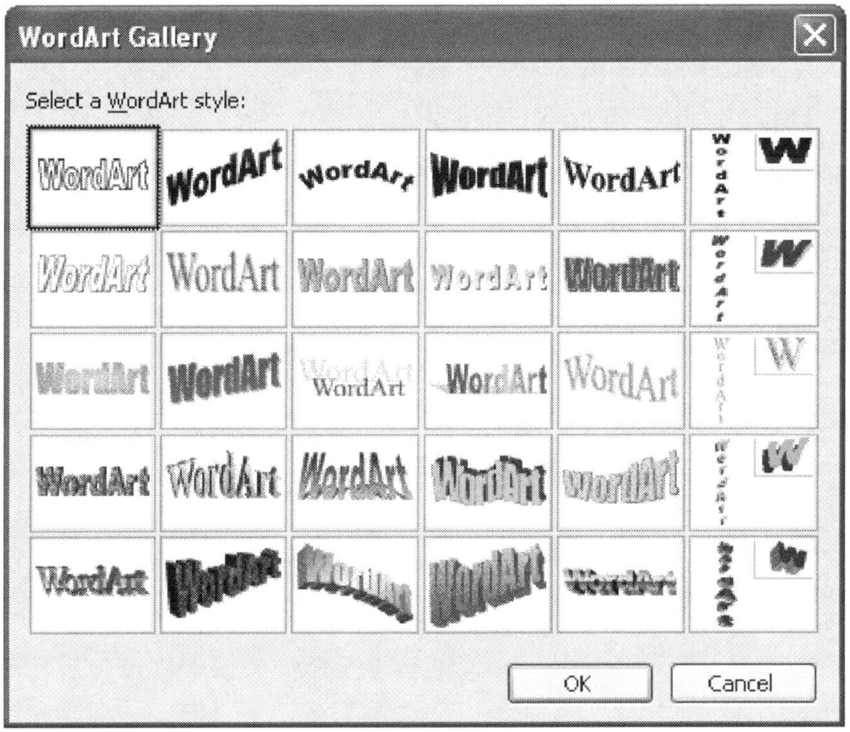

The WordArt Gallery.

3. Select a general appearance that you want used for your text, and then click on OK. You then see the Edit WordArt Text dialog box.

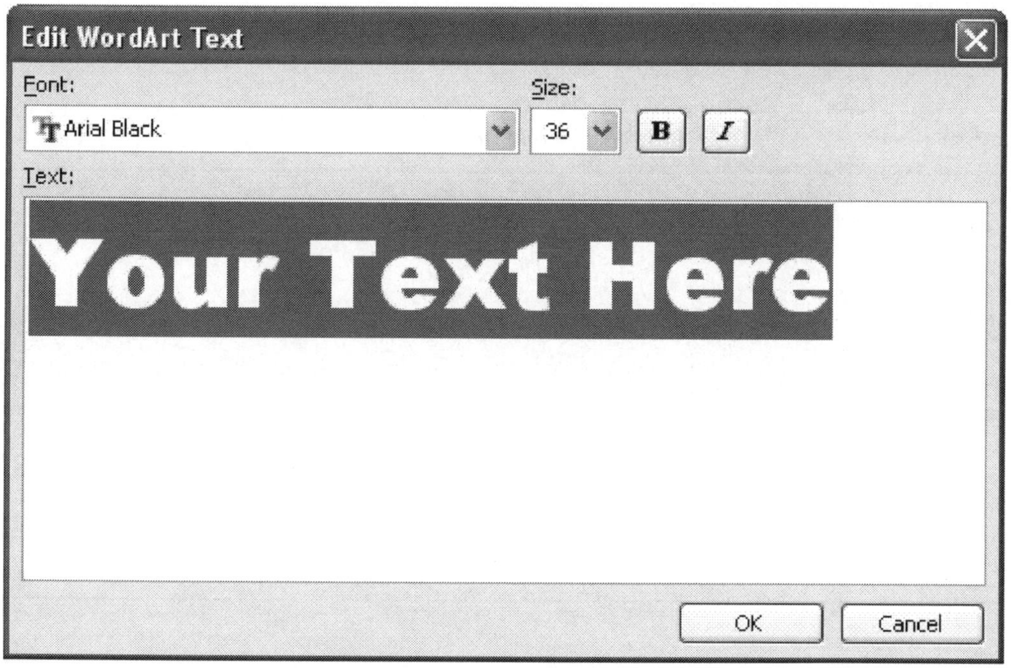

The Edit WordArt Text dialog box.

4. Enter the text you want used by WordArt, and click on OK.

At this point, the WordArt graphic is created and added to your worksheet. You should also see the WordArt toolbar, which includes commands specific to working with WordArt objects. To hide the toolbar, simply click a different place in your document, so that the WordArt object isn't selected.

Specifying a Font in WordArt

WordArt is a program that allows you to treat text as a graphic. You can use the program to add special effects and flourishes to text and then insert the text in your worksheet. It may seem weird to talk about a tool normally associated with Word when discussing Excel, but WordArt works just as well in Excel as it does in Word.

Once you have a WordArt object in your worksheet, you may want to modify it to give it more "pizzazz." By changing the font used by WordArt, you can greatly change the appearance of your WordArt object. To change fonts, follow these general steps:

1. Select the WordArt object by clicking on it. The WordArt toolbar should appear.
2. Click on the Edit Text tool. WordArt displays the Edit WordArt Text dialog box.

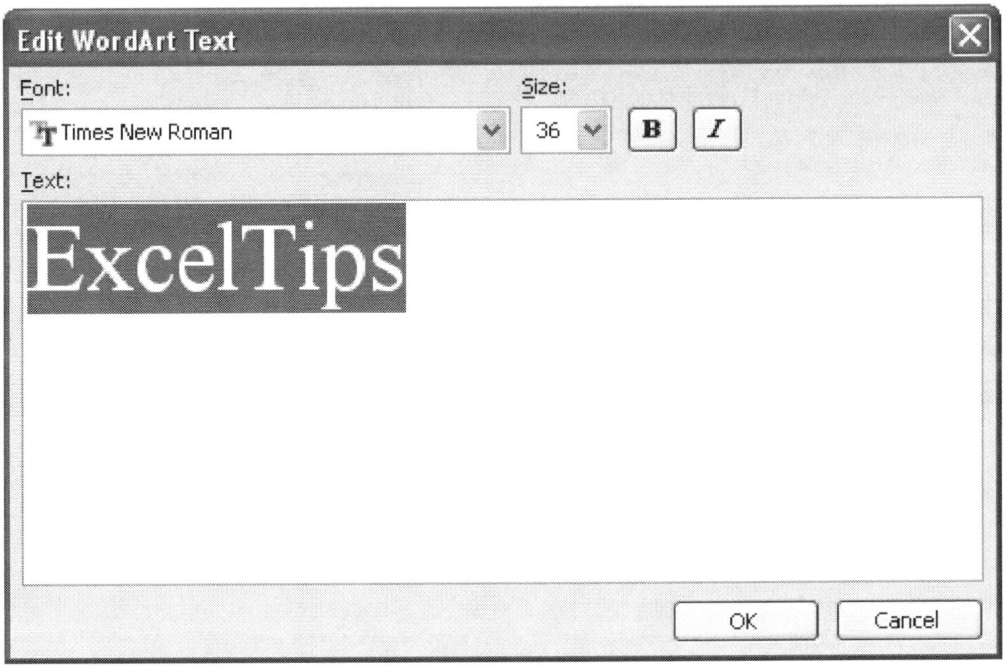

The Edit WordArt Text dialog box.

3. Use the Font pull-down list to select a font to use.
4. Change the font size, as desired.
5. Use Bold or Italics, as desired.
6. Click on OK. WordArt updates your WordArt object.

Adding the Camera

Excel allows you to capture "pictures" of your worksheets that you can use in other worksheets. This may sound odd, but it is quite helpful at times. You capture pictures by using the Camera tool. This tool allows you to capture dynamic "pictures" of different areas of your worksheet.

The Camera tool is not available, by default, on any Excel toolbar. Instead, you need to add it to the toolbar. Follow these steps:

1. Choose Customize from the Tools menu. Excel displays the customize dialog box.
2. Make sure the Commands tab is displayed.

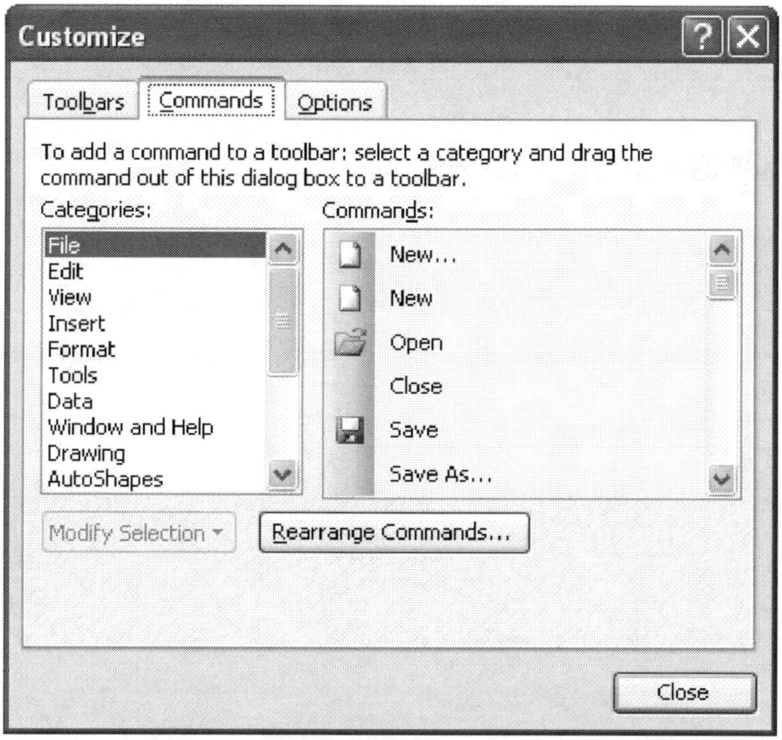

The Commands tab of the Customize dialog box.

3. In the list of Categories, choose Tools, and then scroll through the Commands list until you find Camera. (Oddly enough, it has a small camera icon to the left of the command.)
4. Drag the Camera command to a toolbar and drop it there.
5. Close the Customize dialog box.

You are now ready to use the Camera tool as described in the next tip.

Taking Pictures

Excel allows you to capture "pictures" of your worksheets that you can use in other worksheets. This may sound odd, but it is quite helpful at times. You capture pictures by using the Camera tool. You can customize your toolbars as described in past issues of ***ExcelTips*** to make the camera tool available. (When you are doing your customizing, the Camera tool is available on the Commands tab in the Tools section. It is near the bottom of the list of commands and looks—oddly enough—like a small camera.)

With the Camera tool in place, follow these steps:

1. Select the cells or range of which you want a picture taken.
2. Click on the Camera tool. The mouse pointer changes to a large plus sign.
3. Change to a different worksheet.
4. Click where you want the top left-hand corner of the picture to appear. The picture is inserted as a graphic on the worksheet.

Now you can manipulate the picture the same as you would any other graphic—stretch it, resize it, crop it, move it, or whatever. The really cool thing, however, is that the picture is dynamic. This means that if you change the information in the original range (that you selected in step 1), then the information in the picture changes as well.

Using the Camera in VBA

In other issues of ***ExcelTips*** you learn about using the Camera tool to capture dynamic pictures of different parts of your worksheet. You may have been wondering how to use the same sort of feature from within VBA. The documentation on the issue is not terribly clear, but the following macro shows the general process:

```
Sub DoCamera()
    Dim MyPrompt As String
    Dim MyTitle As String
    Dim UserRange As Range
    Dim OutputRange As Range

    Application.ScreenUpdating = True

    'Prompt user for range to capture
    MyPrompt = "Select the range you would like to capture."
    MyTitle = "User Input Required"
    On Error Resume Next
    Set UserRange = Application.InputBox(Prompt:=MyPrompt, _
        Title:=MyTitle, Default:=ActiveCell.Address, Type:=8)
    If UserRange Is Nothing Then End
    On Error GoTo 0

    'Copy range to Clipboard as picture
    UserRange.CopyPicture

    'Prompt user for range to paste to
    MyPrompt = "Select the range on which you would like to paste."
    MyTitle = "User Input Required"
    On Error Resume Next
    Set OutputRange = Application.InputBox(Prompt:=MyPrompt, _
        Title:=MyTitle, Default:=ActiveCell.Address, Type:=8)
    If OutputRange Is Nothing Then End
    On Error GoTo 0

    'Paste picture to output range
    OutputRange.PasteSpecial
    Selection.Formula = UserRange.Address
End Sub
```

This macro prompts you to specify a range to be copied, it then copies it to the Clipboard as a picture, and prompts you for where to paste it. When pasted, the final line of the macro is the key to making the "photo" dynamic, just as is done manually with the Camera tool. The PasteSpecial command actually pastes the picture, and the pasted picture remains selected. Setting the Formula property for the selection (the picture) results in the dynamic nature of the graphic.

11

Creating Charts

Creating a Chart

When you create a chart using Excel, the value within each cell that is being charted is converted to a ***datapoint,*** which is at the intersection of the X and Y axes for two-dimensional charts or the X, Y, and Z axes for three-dimensional charts. This datapoint can be expressed in any number of chart styles, including bars, columns, lines, and pie wedges.

The easiest way to create a chart is to use the Chart Wizard by following these steps:

1. Select the data range to be charted, or select a single cell within the table you wish to chart. Don't include any summary or total information in the range. You will create the best charts when you work with raw data. You can select any headings, however.
2. Click on the Chart Wizard tool to start the Chart Wizard. This displays the Chart Wizard dialog box, where you are asked to select a chart type.

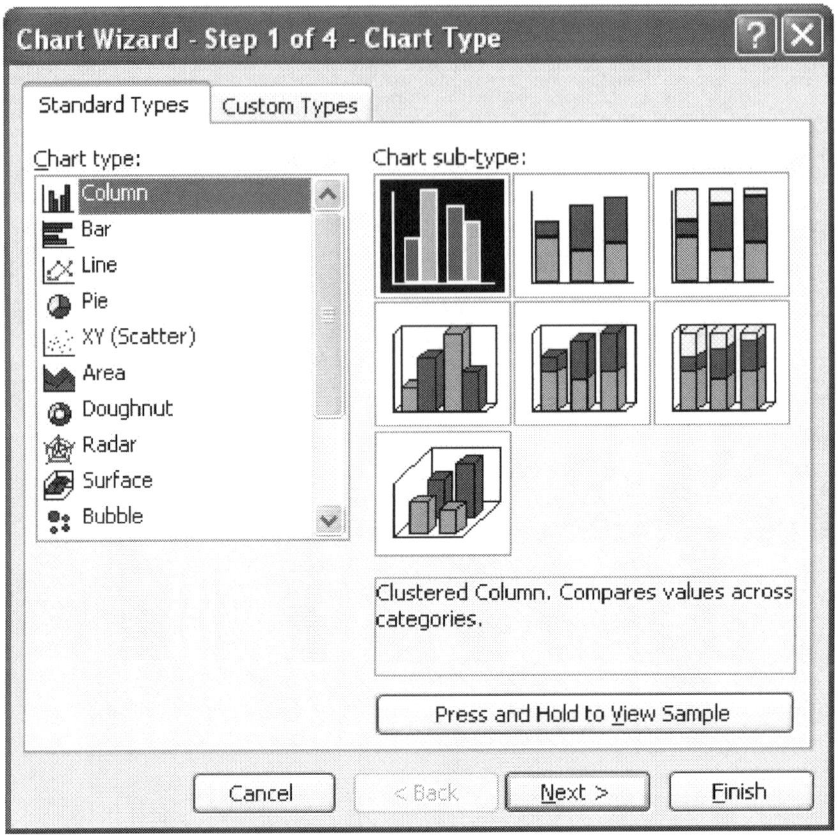

The first step of the Chart Wizard.

3. Select any of the 14 types shown in the Chart Type list. (You can always make changes later.) When you select a type, the information in the Chart Sub-type area of the dialog box is changed.
4. Click on one of the Chart Sub-types shown at the right side of the dialog box.
5. Click on Next. Excel proceeds to the second step of the ChartWizard, where your information is first presented as a chart.
6. Make any necessary changes to the data range depicted in the dialog box, then click on Next. Excel displays the third step of the Chart Wizard.

7. Using the controls in the dialog box, indicate the title, labels, and other formatting you want used for your chart. As you make changes, notice that the sample chart is updated to reflect your changes.
8. When you are happy with your formatting settings, click on the Next button. Excel displays the final step of the ChartWizard. Here you select whether you want your chart embedded in your worksheet or to appear on its own, as a chart sheet.
9. Click on Finish. Your chart is created as you directed.

You should note that these are general steps for using the Chart Wizard. It is possible that the steps may be modified a bit depending on the type of chart you choose to create.

Make that Chart Quickly!

Sometimes going through the Chart Wizards seems to take forever. If you want to put a chart into your workbook very quickly, you can follow these two simple steps:

1. Select the table on which the chart is to be based.
2. Press **F11**.

That's it! Excel inserts a new Chart worksheet before the current worksheet, and bases the chart on the data in your table and the default chart type you have set up. At this point you can perform whatever customization you desire on the chart and work with it as normal.

Creating a Log/Log Chart

Excel is great at automatically creating a wide variety of charts, lickety split. For some types of data, you may want to create a chart that is not readily apparently. Such is the case with a log/log chart.

The answer to this conundrum is to change which type of chart you use for your data. It seems that Excel will not allow the X axis to use a logarithmic scale for many types of charts. To specify a chart where you can use logarithmic scales on both axes, follow these steps:

1. Select the chart area (the actual chart or the spreadsheet area you want to chart).
2. Click the Chart Wizard button on the toolbar.

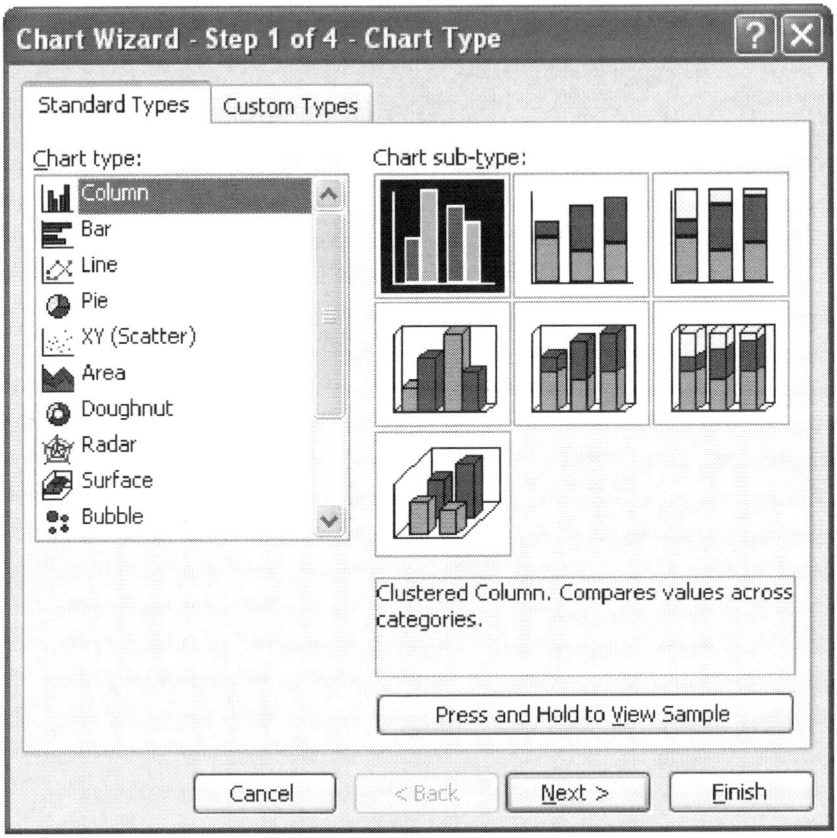

The Chart Wizard.

3. Select the XY (scatter) type of chart.
4. Select the sub-chart type you want to use.
5. Click on the Finish button.

If, for some strange reason, values along the X axis are still not represented in logarithmic scale, you can click on the X axis, choose to format it, and then specify a logarithmic scale.

You should note that this solution will work for many types of charts, but won't work for charts where you need to plot zero or negative values. (Those values don't have a LOG value.)

So why do you need to use a scatter chart for log/log data? Because it is the only type of chart that allows numeric values along the X axis. Other chart types use the X axis for categories of information, not numeric values.

Creating Custom Chart Formats

There may be times when the built-in chart formats just don't meet your needs. In these instances, you can always make any changes desired to your chart and then save all the chart settings as a user-defined format. You can then apply these settings to other charts, and you won't have to go through the long or tedious steps necessary to do all the formatting over again.

To create your own chart format, follow these steps:

1. Use whatever formatting commands are necessary to define your chart just the way you want it.
2. Choose Chart Type from the Chart menu. Excel displays the Chart Type dialog box.
3. Make sure the Custom Types tab is displayed.

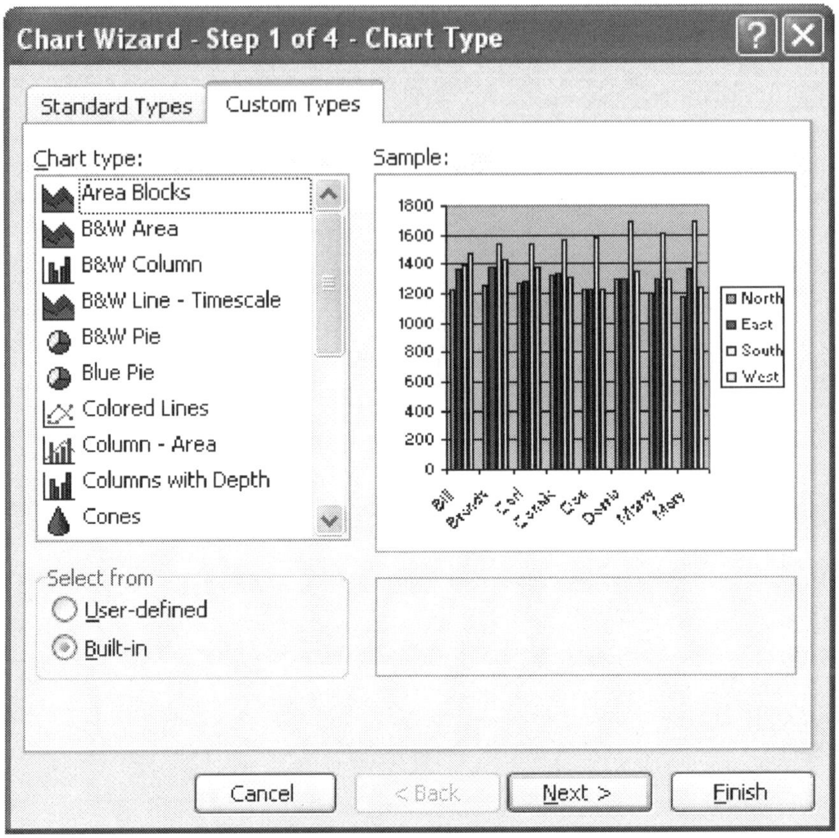

The Custom Types tab of the Chart Type dialog box.

4. Make sure the User-defined option button is selected at the bottom of the dialog box.
5. Click on the Add button. Excel displays the Add Custom Chart Type dialog box.

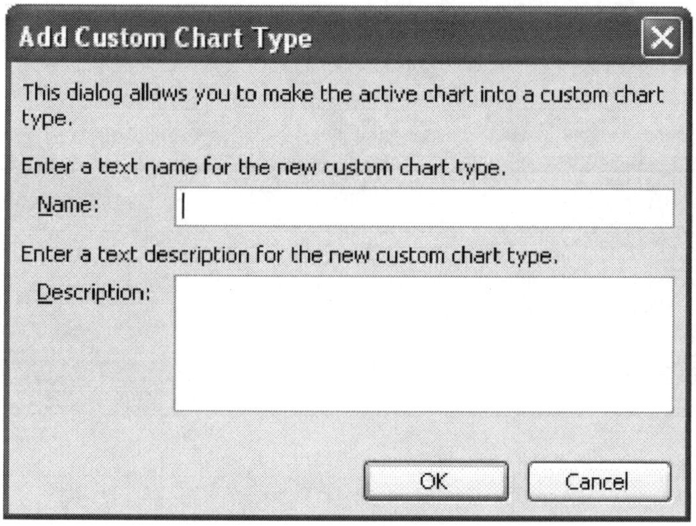

The Add Custom Chart Type dialog box.

6. Enter the name and description that you want assigned to this chart format.
7. Click on OK. The format is saved and is available from the Custom tab of the Chart Types dialog box.

Changing Chart Type

When you create a chart in Excel, the chart can be either embedded as an object within an worksheet, or you can add the chart as its own worksheet. Each type of chart has its advantages, and at some time you might want to change a particular chart from one type to the other. In order to do this, follow these steps:

1. Select the chart you want to change. If working with a chart object, then you should see a series of handles around the perimeter of the chart. If working with a chart sheet, the chart sheet should be displayed.

2. Choose the Location option from the Chart menu. Excel displays the Chart Location dialog box.

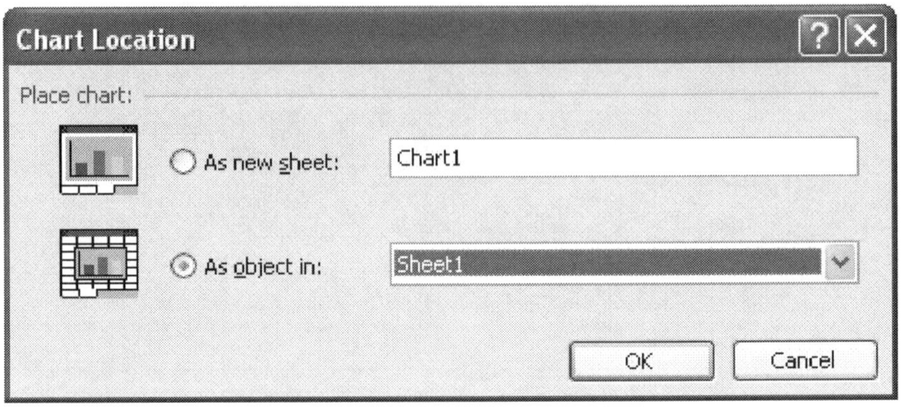

The Chart Location dialog box.

3. Choose whether you want the chart displayed as a sheet or as an object.
4. If you choose that you want the chart displayed as an object, use the drop-down list to select the worksheet on which the chart object should appear.
5. Click on OK.

Using Go To to Jump to a Chart Sheet

When you want to jump to a specific worksheet in a workbook, you can use the Go To feature of Excel to make the jump painless, in the following manner:

1. Press **F5**. Excel displays the Go To dialog box.

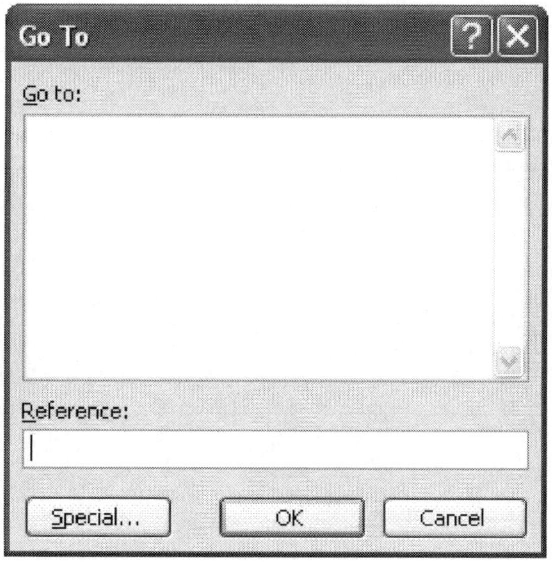

The Go To dialog box.

2. In the Reference box, enter **MySheet!A1**. (Replace "MySheet" with the name of the worksheet you want to jump to.)
3. Click OK.

This works great for regular worksheets, but it won't work if you want to jump to a chart sheet. Why? Because Go To is used to jump to specific cells (in this case, cell A1 on MySheet), and chart sheets have no cells you can reference.

If you want a quick way to jump to a chart sheet, you will need to resort to a macro. You can have the macro ask for a chart sheet name, and then use the Activate or Select methods with the sheet name. The pertinent line of the macro—the one that does the actual "jumping"—can be either of these:

```
Sheets("MyChart").Activate
Sheets("MyChart").Select
```

All you need to do is substitute the proper name of the chart sheet in place of "MyChart."

Controlling Chart Gridlines

When you create a chart from your Excel data, the Chart Wizard takes care of many of the actual details related to how a specific chart appears. One of the elements that can be included on many of the charts is gridlines. Gridlines are helpful for easily determining the height or width of graphic elements used in your chart.

Excel allows you to specifically control which gridlines are displayed, or if they are displayed at all. You can do so by following these steps:

1. Select the chart by clicking on it. You should see selection handles appear around the outside of the chart.
2. Choose Chart Options from the Chart menu. Excel displays the Chart Options dialog box.
3. Make sure the Gridlines tab is displayed. The settings on this tab control which gridlines are displayed in your chart. The actual settings available depend on the type of chart format you are using.

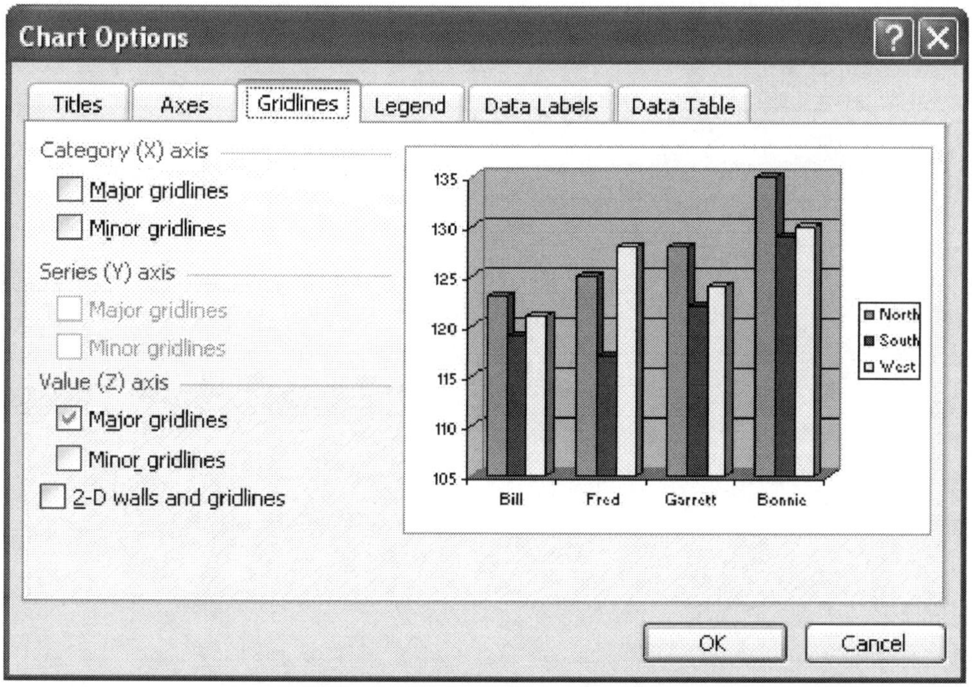

The Gridlines tab of the Chart Options dialog box.

4. Change the settings, as desired.
5. Click on OK. The chart is updated to reflect your choice.

12

Modifying and Formatting Charts

Selecting Fonts for a Chart

When creating a chart in Excel, you can add various elements to the charts, such as titles or data labels. Excel allows you to change the font used to display these elements, if you desire. You can change fonts for these elements individually. To do this, use these steps:

1. Make sure your chart is visible on the screen and you have selected it. (You do this by clicking on the chart.)
2. Select the text element whose font you wish to change. For instance, if you want to change the chart's title, click on the title. Excel displays small black squares around the element; this lets you know it is selected.
3. Choose Selected from the Format menu. (The word "Selected" in the menu will be followed by the type of object you selected, as in "Selected Chart Title.") Excel displays the Format dialog box for the element.
4. Make sure the Font tab is selected.

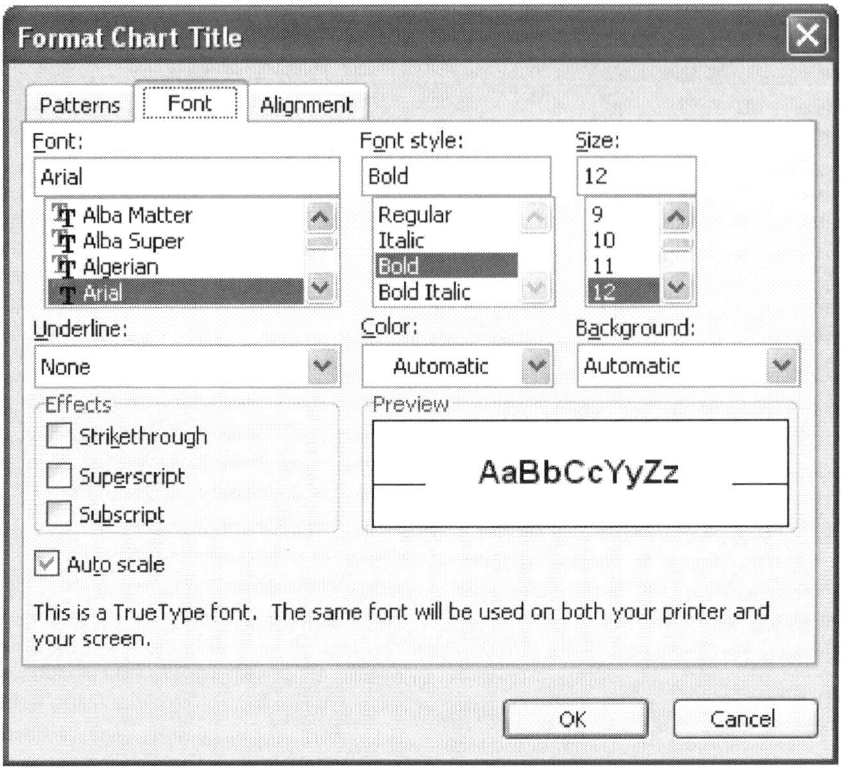

The Font tab of the Format Chart Title dialog box.

5. Change the font settings, as desired.
6. Click on OK.

Unselecting a Chart Item

Excel includes a very powerful charting feature. As you work with charting your data, it is not unusual to select different objects and then use the various formatting features of Excel to make that object look exactly as you want it to. You select chart objects by simply clicking on the object with the mouse.

If you select an object by mistake, you can easily undo that selection by simply selecting a different object. If you don't want to select a different object, but instead want to "deselect" the item you selected, all you need to do is press the **Esc** key. Excel obediently cancels whatever selection you made.

Using the Keyboard to Select and Resize a Chart Object

Charts can be included in a workbook in one of two ways: as chart sheets or as chart objects. A chart sheet means that the chart takes up its own sheet in the workbook. A chart object appears as an object in a regular worksheet.

If you like to use the keyboard in preference to the mouse, you may wonder how you can select and resize a chart object. There are a couple of ways to approach the problem, depending on your version of Excel. The methods are rather, shall we say, messy—they involve quite a few steps. These will work in Excel 97 or Excel 2000:

1. Make sure the Drawing toolbar is displayed.
2. Press **F10** or the **Alt** key to activate the menu bar. (The File menu will be selected.)
3. Repeatedly press **Ctrl+Tab** or **Ctrl+Shift+Tab** (as necessary) until the Drawing toolbar is selected.
4. Repeatedly press the arrow keys until the Select Objects tool (the one that looks like a mouse pointer) is selected.
5. Press **Enter**. The Select Objects tool is now activated.
6. Repeatedly press **Tab** or **Shift+Tab** (as necessary) until handles appear around the chart object.
7. Press **Alt+O** to display the Format menu.
8. Use the arrow keys to select the Object option from the menu and press **Enter**. Excel displays the Format Object dialog box.
9. Use the **Tab** key and arrow keys to adjust the various size options in the dialog box.
10. Press **Enter** to accept your changes and close the dialog box.
11. Press **Esc** to de-activate the Select Objects tool on the Drawing toolbar and return to the worksheet.

If you are using Excel 2002 or Excel 2003, following the above steps will cause Excel to crash. (At least, it did on my system.) This is very interesting; the crash occurs every time at step 6. If you are using Excel 2002 or Excel 2003 you should follow these steps, instead:

1. Make sure the Drawing toolbar is displayed.
2. Press **F10** or the **Alt** key to activate the menu bar. (The File menu will be selected.)
3. Repeatedly press **Ctrl+Tab** or **Ctrl+Shift+Tab** (as necessary) until the Drawing toolbar is selected.
4. Repeatedly press the arrow keys until the Select Objects tool (the one that looks like a mouse pointer) is selected.
5. Press **Ctrl+Enter**. Excel selects the first object in the worksheet, which in all likelihood is your chart object.
6. Press **Alt+O** to display the Format menu.
7. Use the arrow keys to select the Object option from the menu and press **Enter**. Excel displays the Format Object dialog box.
8. Use the **Tab** key and arrow keys to adjust the various size options in the dialog box.
9. Press **Enter** to accept your changes and close the dialog box.
10. Press **Esc** to de-activate the Select Objects tool on the Drawing toolbar and return to the worksheet.

Obviously, using the mouse to resize a chart object would be much easier. If you need to use the keyboard extensively to duplicate what is normally done with the mouse, you might consider using the Mouse Keys accessibility feature of Windows. Exactly how you use this feature is beyond the scope of ExcelTips, but it allows you to regain much of the convenience of the mouse by simply using the keyboard. You can install this feature by checking out the Accessibility applet in the Control Panel.

Colorizing Charts

If you have a pie chart with a large number of sections, getting unique colors for each section might be a problem. Or, perhaps your printer doesn't print colors exactly as they are on your screen so some colors that appear quite distinct on the screen print out nearly the same on paper.

Don't despair—you can change the color of any individual section of a pie chart, or any other type of chart for that matter. For pie charts, follow these steps:

1. Click on the "pie" so that it is surrounded by handles (little squares).
2. Click again on the section you want to change. The handles will now surround only that section.
3. Right-click on the section. Excel displays a Context menu.
4. Choose the Format Data Point option from the Context menu. Excel displays the Format Data Point dialog box, with the Patterns tab selected.

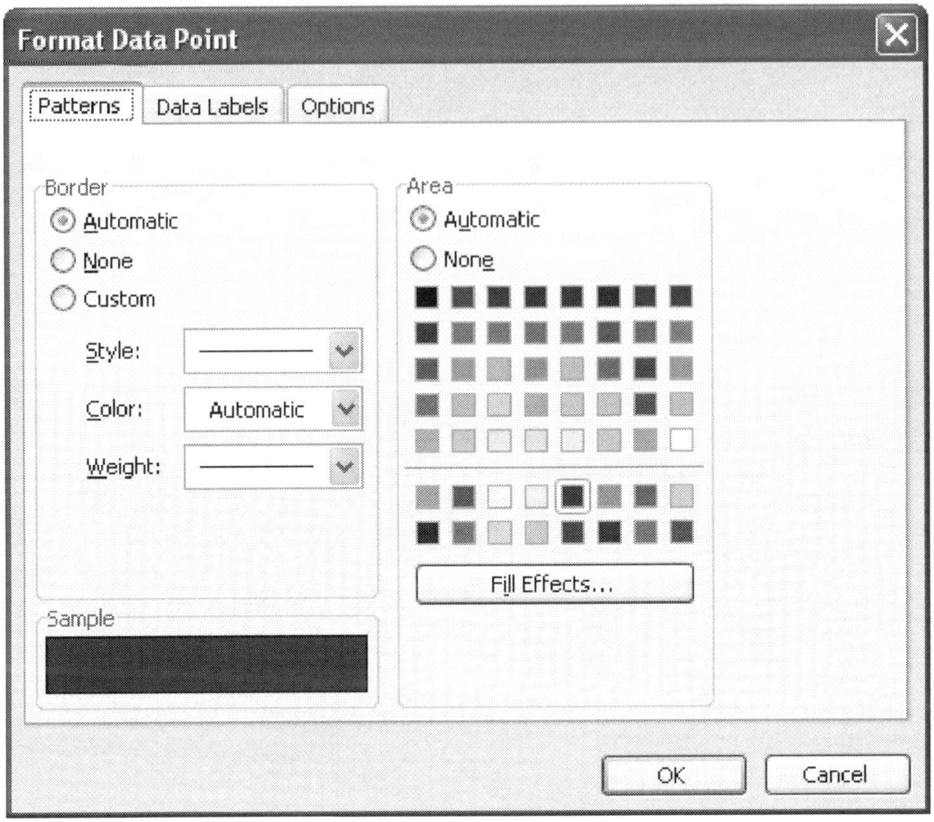

The Format Data Point dialog box.

5. In the Area portion of the dialog box, select the color you want to use for the chart section.
6. Click on OK. Excel updates your chart.

These steps can be easily adapted to any type of chart. The only difference is that you select the chart object (bar, point, what have you) in the first two steps instead of the pie section.

When I make a chart, I also like to apply this same process to chart titles. I like them to be the same color as the information in the chart to which they apply. This makes identification even clearer.

Changing Chart Types

Excel makes changing chart types of an existing chart a breeze. You can change chart types by following these steps:

1. Select the chart you want to change. You do this by clicking on the chart, if you are selecting an embedded chart. (Eight handles appear around the perimeter of the chart.) If you are selecting a chart sheet, simply make sure the sheet is displayed.
2. Choose the Chart Type option from the Chart menu. Excel displays the Chart Type dialog box. This dialog box looks very similar to one of the steps in the Chart Wizard. Notice that the current chart type is highlighted in the dialog box.

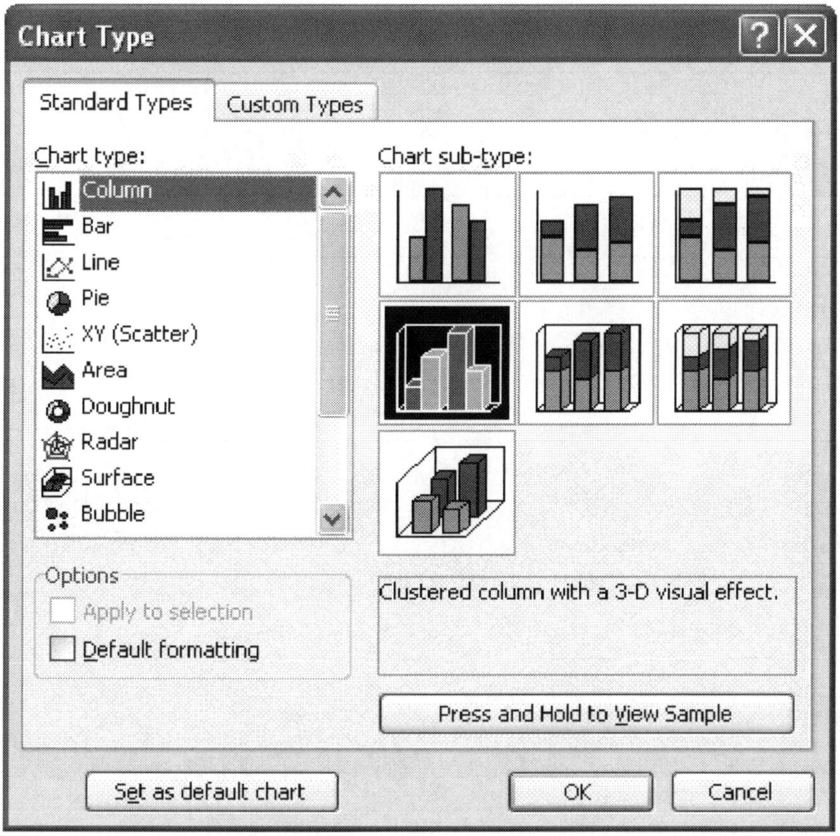

The Chart Type dialog box.

3. Select any of the major chart types shown in the Chart Type list. When you select a type, the information in the Chart Sub-type area of the dialog box is changed.
4. Click on one of the Chart Sub-types shown at the right side of the dialog box.
5. Click on the OK button. Your chart is reformatted using the chart type and sub-type you selected.

Changing Chart Size

There are two types of charts that you can create in Excel—embedded charts and chart sheets. A chart sheet occupies an entire page. An embedded chart appears on the same page as your worksheet data.

If you are working with an embedded chart, you can change the size of the chart to any size you want. You cannot directly change the size of a chart sheet; it is set to be a single page. You can modify the printed size of a chart sheet, however. (This is covered in a different ***ExcelTip***.)

You change the size of an embedded chart as you would any other graphical object in Excel:

1. Click once on the chart. Handles appear around the chart border. As you move the mouse pointer over these handles, they change to sizing arrows.
2. Click and hold the left mouse button and drag a sizing handle until the graphic is the size you want. The arrow heads on the mouse pointer indicate the direction which you can move the border.
3. Release the mouse button. The chart is resized and reformatted.

Controlling the Plotting of Empty Cells

When you create a chart from a data table, Excel does its best to translate the numeric values into data points on a chart, according to the specifications you provide. One area where Excel doesn't quite know what to do, however, is empty cells. If a cell is empty, it could be for any number of reasons—the value isn't available, the value isn't important, or the value is really zero.

You can instruct the program how you want it to treat empty cells by following these steps:

1. Select the chart you want to affect.
2. Choose Options from the Tools menu. Excel displays the Options dialog box.
3. Make sure the Chart tab is displayed.

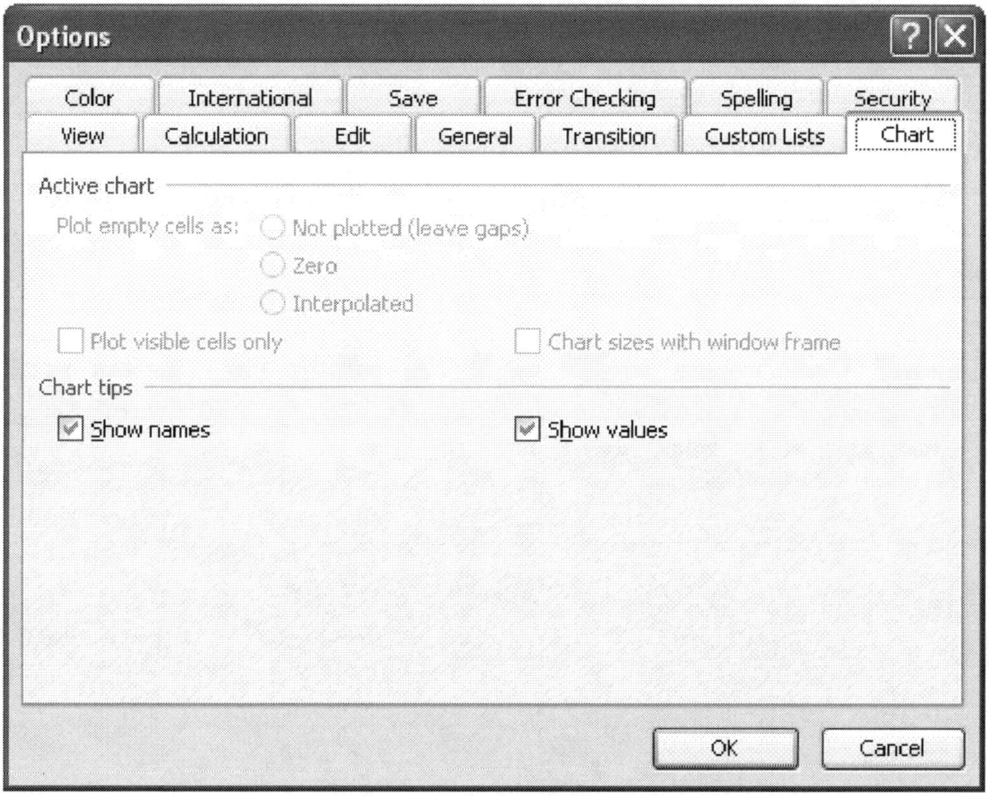

The Chart tab of the Options dialog box.

4. Using the option buttons at the top of the dialog box, specify how you want Excel to chart empty cells.
5. Click OK.

If the option buttons are not available at the top of the screen, it means that you don't have a chart visible on the screen. The option buttons provide three different settings:

- **Not Plotted.** Excel leaves gaps in the chart where the empty cells appear.
- **Zero.** Excel treats the empty cells as if they contained zero values, and plots accordingly.
- **Interpolated.** Excel examines the values surrounding the empty cell and guesses what value the cell should contain based on those values.

Using Chart Titles

Pretty graphics in a chart may look nice at first, but graphics alone seldom convey the entire message desired. Without ***titles***, many charts would be cryptic at best and useless at worst. Titles add purpose and meaning to your chart. Excel allows you to add several different types of titles.

You should note that the titles available for any given chart will vary, depending on the type of chart you are using. For instance, the only type of title available with a pie chart is the chart title itself. Since there are no X, Y, and Z axes on a pie chart, there are no titles available for them.

To insert titles, follow these steps:

1. Activate the chart by clicking on it, if necessary.
2. Choose Chart Options from the Chart menu. Excel displays the Chart Options dialog box.
3. Make sure the Titles tab is selected.

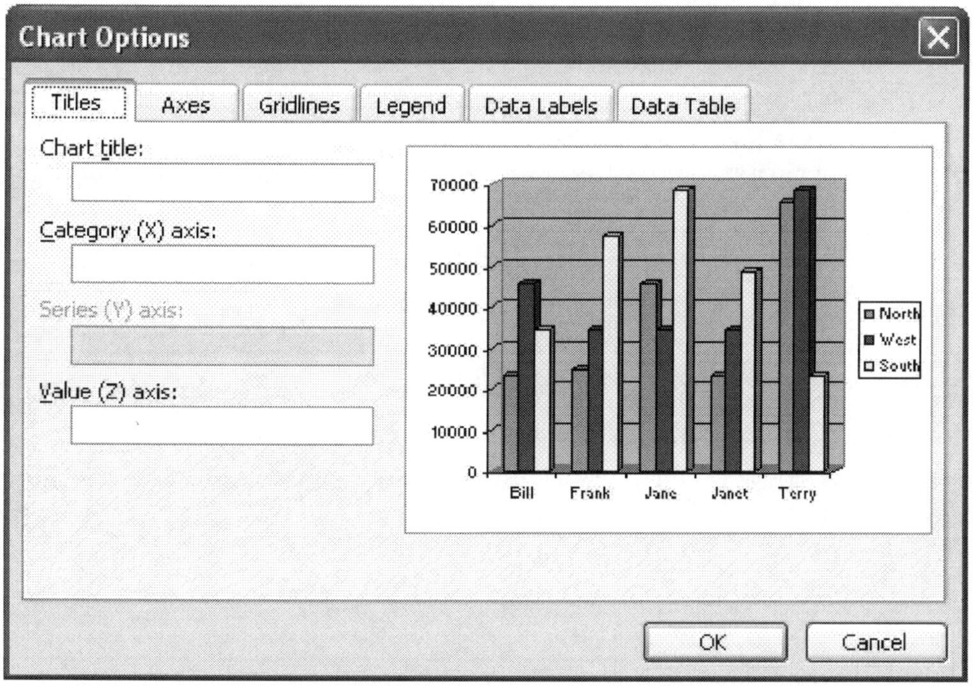

The Titles tab of the Chart Options dialog box.

4. Fill in the appropriate fields in the dialog box for the titles you wish to add. If you leave a field blank, the title will not be included.
5. When finished, click on OK. The titles are updated as you directed.

To change the text contained within a title, you can always follow these same steps again. There is an easier, more direct way to change title text, however. All you need to do is click on the title. The title is selected and surrounded with a box and handles. When you move the mouse pointer inside the box, it changes to an insertion point. Click the mouse pointer once to edit the text.

Notice that if you press **Enter**, the cursor only moves to the next line; you are still adding to the title. To signify that you are finished entering title text, you must use the mouse pointer to select some other part of your chart or worksheet.

When you add titles to your chart, Excel places them in a position it feels is best for the title. Thus, an axis title will be centered on the axis. You can move titles very easily, however. To do this, use the mouse to select the title text. When you do, it becomes surrounded with a box and handles. Use the mouse to point to the border around the title. Press and hold down the mouse button. As you move the mouse, the title is also moved. When you release the mouse button, the title remains at the new location.

Using Dynamic Chart Titles

There is a very cool way, apparently not well known, of adding 'active' or 'live' titles and other text to charts. In this way you can make a change in a worksheet and have that change reflected in a title in the chart. Follow these steps:

1. Create your chart as you normally would.
2. Add whatever titles, datapoints, axis names, etc. are desired.
3. Select the title you want to modify. Small handles should appear around the title.
4. In the Formula bar enter the address of the cell you want to use for the title. For instance, if the title is in cell A1 of the MySheet worksheet, you would enter the following in the formula bar:

```
=MySheet!$A$1
```

That's it. Now, whenever the contents of A1 are changed Excel updates the information in the chart's title.

Turning the Legend On and Off

When you create a chart in Excel, the Wizard that you follow may create a chart legend, depending on the type of chart you are using. You are not limited to the Wizard's decision, however. You have complete control over whether a legend is displayed on your chart. Follow these steps:

1. Click once on the legend to select it. Handles should appear around the perimeter of the legend.
2. Choose Chart Options from the Chart menu. Excel displays the Chart Options dialog box.

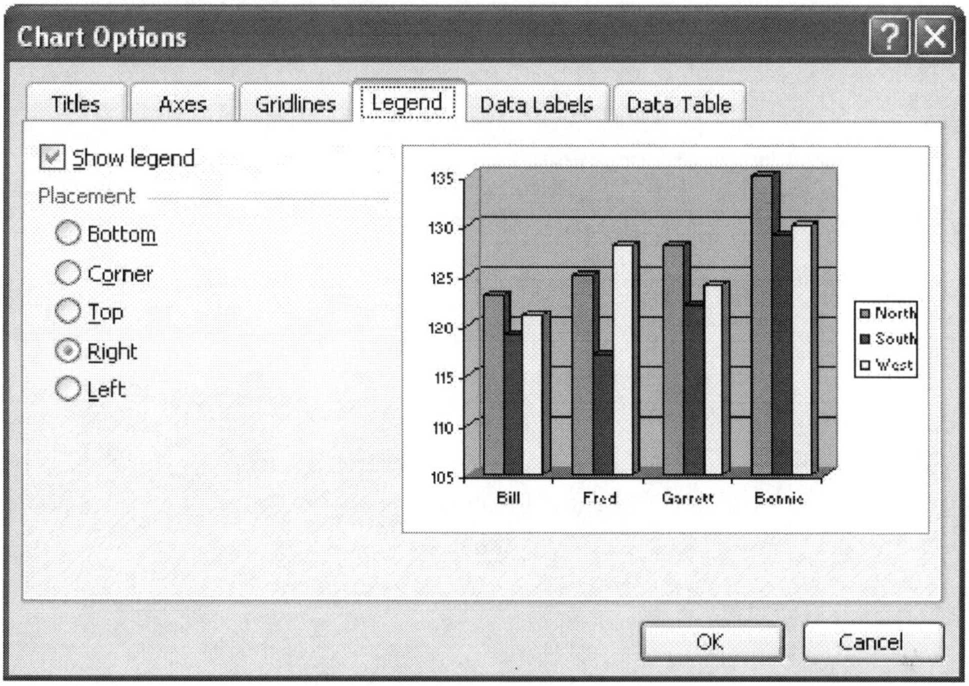

The Chart Options dialog box.

3. Make sure the Legend tab is selected.
4. Clear the Show Legend check box.
5. Click on OK.

Moving a Chart's Legend

Excel provides a wide range of charts you can use to graphically represent the data in your worksheet. The provided charts are just a start, however, as you can modify the base charts quite a bit. For instance, you can add a legend to your chart, as described in other issues of ***ExcelTips.*** Once your legend is placed, your options are still not complete. You can move the legend to any position within your chart.

To move a chart's legend, simply click on it once to select it. (You will know it is selected when eight handles appear around the perimeter of the legend.) Then use the mouse to click within the legend and drag the legend to the desired position on the chart. When you release the mouse button, the legend stays were you dropped it.

Putting a Chart Legend On Its Own Page

Lorna wonders if it is possible to put the legend associated with a chart onto a different page than the chart itself. She is submitting a paper to a journal that wants them separated.

The short answer is that Excel has made the legend and the chart integral to each other and there is not a quick and easy way to separate the two. There is a way to trick Excel into thinking that both elements exist, however. You start to do this may making an additional copy of the chart:

1. Select the chart.
2. Select File | Copy or **Ctrl+C**. Excel copies the chart.
3. Click in the area you want the legend to appear.
4. Select File | Paste of **Ctrl+V**. Excel pastes the chart.

You now have two copies of the chart. One will be used for the actual chart (Chart 1) and the other chart (Chart 2) will be the legend. Hiding the legend from Chart 1 is simple and can be accomplished as follows:

1. Single click on the chart.
2. Select Chart | Chart Options. Excel displays the Chart Options dialog box.
3. Click on the Legends tab.

4. Clear the Show Legend check box.
5. Click OK.

The legend no longer appears with the chart. But you have only solved half of the problem. Now you need to work with Chart 2 and isolate the legend on its own page. There are a couple of options to do this.

One option is to use screen capture to obtain a separate image of the legend. For this method, you will need to use a graphics program to trim the image (so it contains just the legend) before placing it back into Excel. Create the chart as usual, then follow these general steps:

1. Use whatever method you prefer to create a screen capture of the legend portion of the chart.
2. Using a graphics program, such as Paint or Adobe Illustrator, trim the image so it contains only the legend.
3. In Excel select Insert | Picture | From File. Excel displays the Insert Picture dialog box.
4. Select the file you created in step 2.
5. Click Insert. The image appears on your worksheet.

At this point, the legend is a simple picture and can be moved to any location you desire.

Another option involves "hiding" the chart so the only visible item in Chart 2 is the legend.

1. Click on Chart 2 so it is selected.
2. Single click on the X-axis line.
3. Select Format | Selected Axis. Excel displays the Format Axis dialog box.
4. Click the Patterns tab.

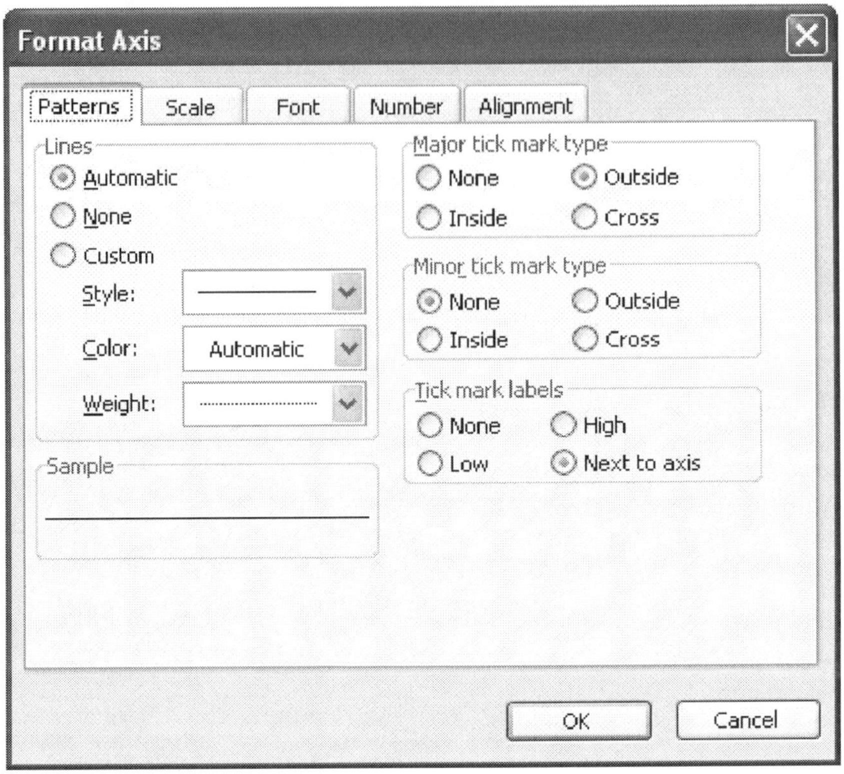

The Patterns tab of the Format Axis dialog box.

5. Select None on all of the options.
6. Click OK. The numbers on the X-axis are removed.
7. Single click on the Y-axis line.
8. Repeat steps 3-5 for the Y-axis.
9. Click OK. The numbers on the Y-axis are removed.
10. Single click on the plot area of the chart.
11. Select Format | Selected Plot Area. Excel displays the Format Plot Area dialog box.

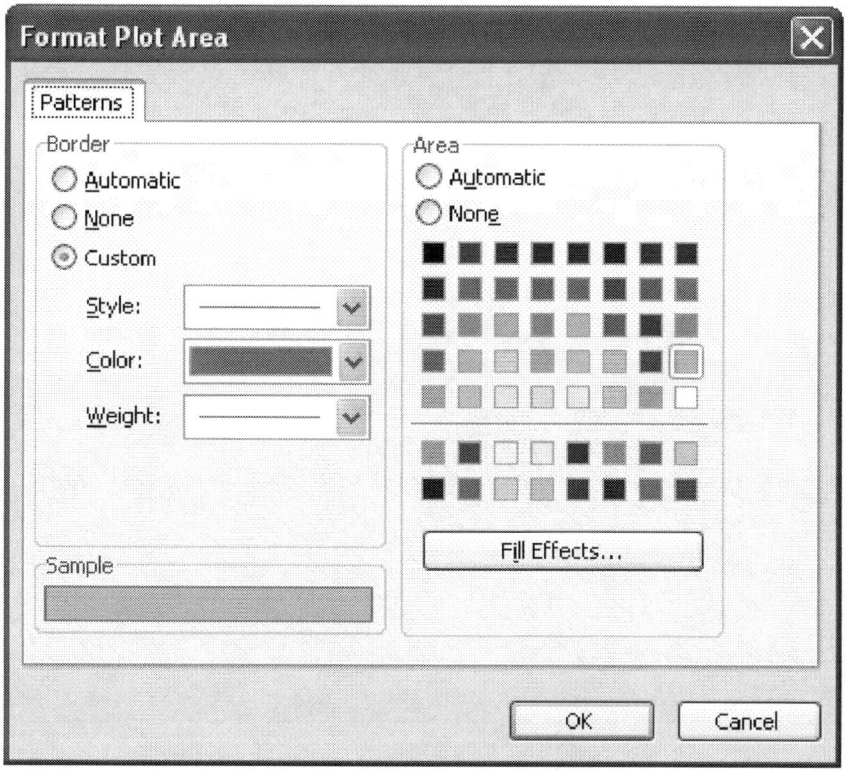

The Format Plot Area dialog box.

12. Select None in the Border and Area sections of the dialog box.
13. Click OK. The border and background of the chart are removed.
14. Single click on one of the horizontal gridlines. Excel selects all of the lines.
15. Select Format | Selected Gridlines. Excel displays the Format Gridlines dialog box.

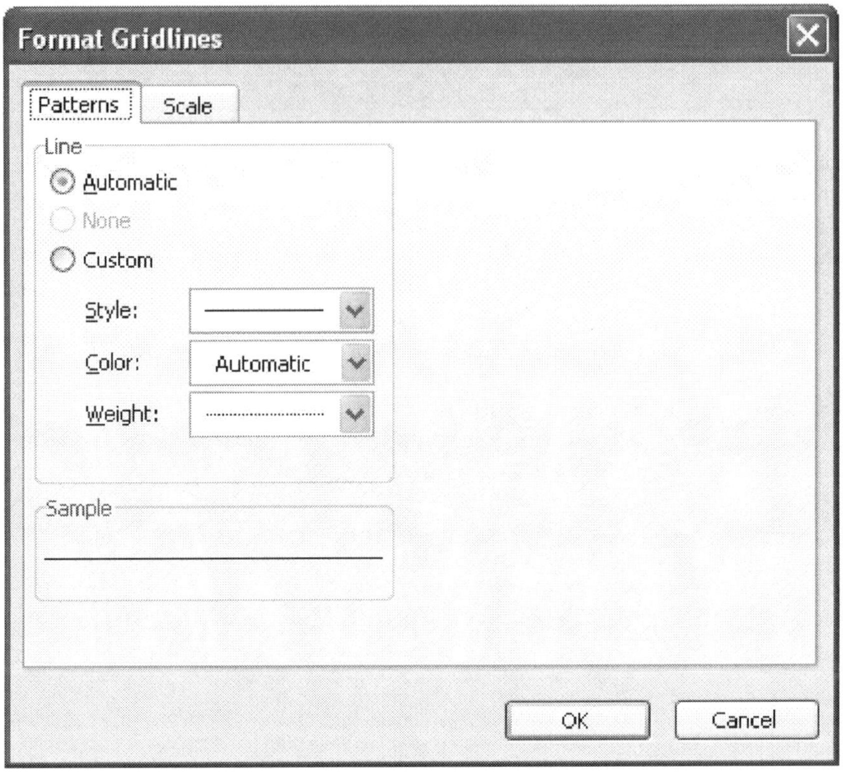

The Format Gridlines dialog box.

16. Select Custom and change the color to white.
17. Click OK. The gridlines are removed and the only remaining portion of the chart is the colored plots.
18. Single click on the plot area.
19. Select Format | Selected Data Series. Excel displays the Format Data Series dialog box.

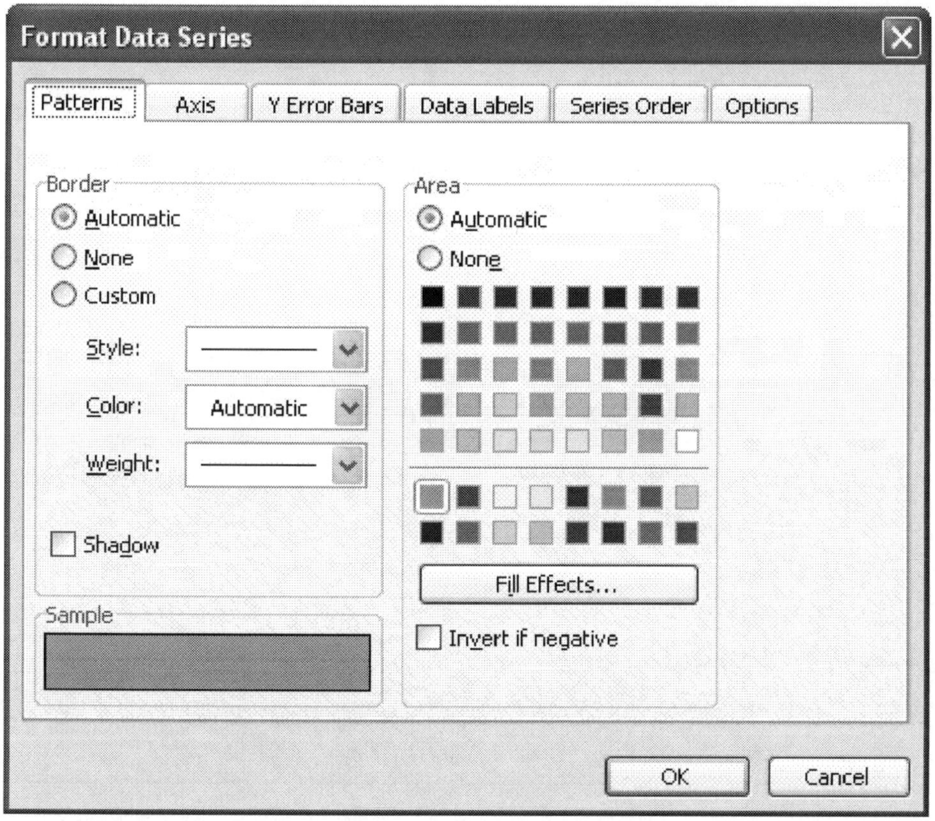

The Format Data Series dialog box.

20. Select None for the Border and Area.
21. Click OK. Excel has "hidden" the chart.

The only element visible at this point is the legend. Keep in mind that the chart is still there, it has just been "hidden" by changing its appearance. This is a long workaround but it gets the job done.

Formatting the Border of a Legend

When you create a chart in Excel, the Wizard that you follow may create a chart legend, depending on the type of chart you are creating. Normally, the appearance of the legend will be acceptable for the type of chart you are creating. You have complete control, however, over how the legend appears.

One of the elements you can change is the type of border Excel places around the legend. To change the appearance of the legend's border, follow these steps:

1. Click once on the legend to select it. Handles should appear around the perimeter of the legend.
2. Choose Selected Legend from the Format menu. Excel displays the Format Legend dialog box.
3. Make sure the Patterns tab is selected.

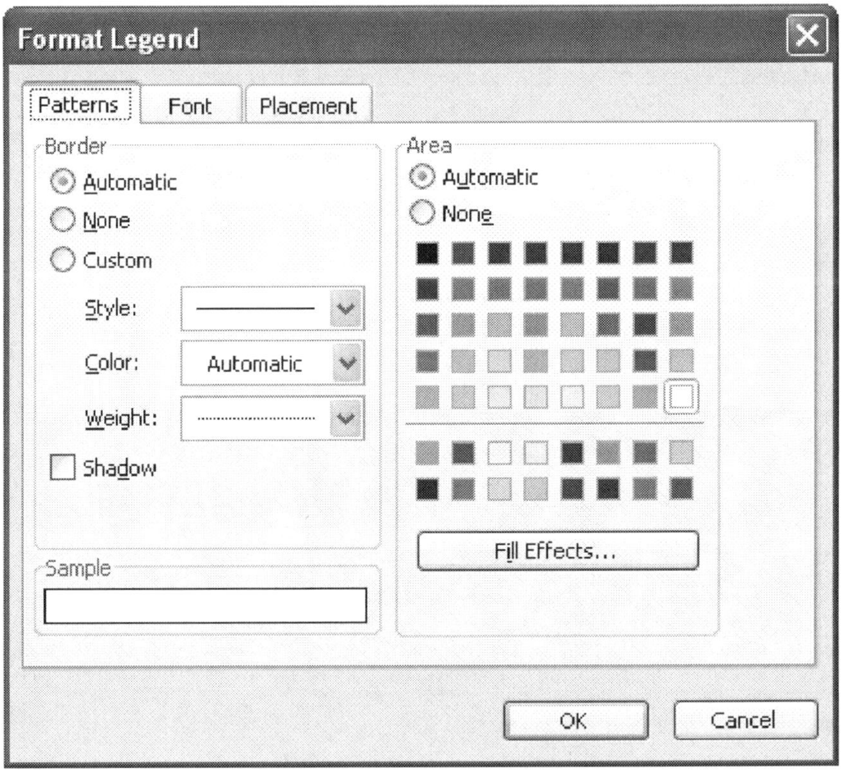

The Patterns tab of the Format Legend dialog box.

4. Use the Style drop-down list to select a different border style for the legend.

5. Use the Color drop-down list to change the color of the border.
6. Use the Weight drop-down list to specify how heavy the border should appear.
7. Use the Shadow check box to control if Excel adds a drop-shadow to the legend.
8. Click on OK.

Adding Data Labels to Your Chart

Data labels are used to indicate what the main part of the chart represents. Depending on the type of chart you are creating, data labels can mean quite a bit. For instance, if you are formatting a pie chart, the data can be more difficult to understand if you don't include data labels.

To add data labels, follow these steps:

1. Activate the chart by clicking on it, if necessary.
2. Choose Chart Options from the Chart menu. Excel displays the Chart Options dialog box.
3. Make sure the Data Labels tab is selected. The left side of the dialog box shows the different types of data labels you can choose. (The available types will vary, depending on the type of chart you are using.)

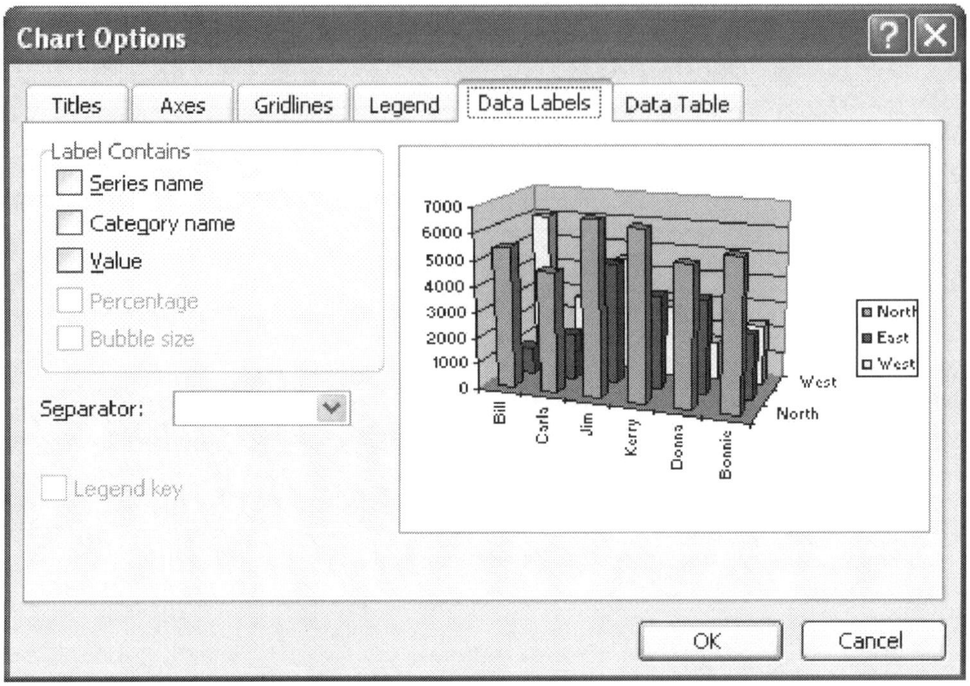

The Data Labels tab of the Chart Options dialog box.

4. There are five different basic types of data labels from which you can choose. Each of them represents a different combination of using the data value, a percentage, or a label as the actual data label. Select the option that best reflects what you want to do. As you make choices, notice that the preview chart is updated according to your selections.
5. Click on OK. Your chart is updated as you directed.

Labeling X-Y Scatter Plots

Martin has a worksheet containing 50 rows of data, each row describing a single object. Column A contains the name of the object, column B contains its X coordinate, and column C contains its Y coordinate. When he creates an X-Y scatter chart (column B against column C) the result, as desired, is a graph showing an array of points showing the location of the objects. However, Martin can't seem to label the data points with their individual names (from column A). When he tries to label the data points the only available options are to label each point with its X value, Y value, or Series Name. Martin wonders if there is a way he can easily use Column A to label the plotted data points.

This can be done manually, but it is tedious at best. For 50 rows it would quickly be brutal, so it is best to look at a macro-oriented approach. One idea is to use a macro similar to the following, which steps through the data points in the X-Y chart and reads the label values from column A.

```
Sub DataLabelsFromRange()
    Dim Cht As Chart
    Dim i, ptcnt As Integer

    Set Cht = ActiveSheet.ChartObjects(1).Chart
    On Error Resume Next
    Cht.SeriesCollection(1).ApplyDataLabels _
      Type:=xlDataLabelsShowValue, _
      AutoText:=True, _
      LegendKey:=False

    ptcnt = Cht.SeriesCollection(1).Points.Count
    For i = 1 To ptcnt
        Cht.SeriesCollection(1).Points(i).DataLabel.Text = _
          ActiveSheet.Cells(i + 1, 1).Value
    Next i
End Sub
```

The macro assumes that the first row of the worksheet contains header information and that the actual data begins in row 2. If the data really begins in row 1, then change "i + 1" to simply "i". (This macro approach is actually a variation of a macro found on pages 570-571 of John Walkenbach's excellent book ***Excel 2003 Power Programming With VBA***.)

One rather unique non-macro approach is to use Excel's custom formats. All you need to do is set up a bunch of custom formats that contain only the text you want to be displayed. For example, if you have the values Age, 15, and 23 in cells A3 to C3, you can format either cell B3 or C3 to show the word "Age" even though the value will remain 15 or 23, respectively. Just enter "Age" (including the quotation marks) for the Custom format for the cell. Then format the chart to display the label for X or Y value.

When you do this, the X-axis values of the chart will probably all changed to whatever the format name is (i.e., Age). However, after formatting the X-axis to

Number (with no digits after the decimal in this case) rather than General, the chart should display correctly.

This approach can obviously still take a bit of time to implement as you set up and apply a bunch of custom formats for each value in your data series. If you don't want to mess with writing and testing your own macros or creating a bunch of custom formats, you can always turn to add-ins written by others. Microsoft MVP Rob Bovey has created an excellent (free) add-in for Excel which includes an X-Y labeling feature among several others. It can be downloaded at this address:

```
http://www.appspro.com/Utilities/ChartLabeler.htm
```

Locking Callouts to a Graph Location

After creating a chart in Excel, you may want to add a callout or two to the chart. For instance, there may be a spike or an anomaly in the data, and you want to include a callout that explains the aberration.

Callouts, when drawn using the Drawing toolbar, are graphic objects that have a "connector" that can point where you want it. This makes them great for pointing to the aberration you want explained in your chart. The problem is, if you change the data range displayed in the charge, the perspective of the charge changes, and the callout no longer points to where it used to point. (It still points to where the aberration used to appear on the chart.)

The reason for this is that the callout and the chart are not related. The callout isn't locked to a specific place on the chart; it just overlays the chart to give the desired effect. There is no way in Excel to link a callout to a specific chart point.

Most people use a different approach to adding explanatory text to their charts. Instead of using a callout, they use data labels to achieve the same purpose. Follow these steps:

1. On the chart, select the data point that you want a "callout" associated with. The first time you click the point, the entire data series is selected. Once the series is selected, wait a moment and then click the same

data point again. This time, only the single data point is selected, not the entire series.

2. Right-click the selected data point and choose Format Data Point from the resulting Context menu. Excel displays the Format Data Point dialog box. (If you don't see the Format Data Point option on the Context menu, it means you didn't select only the single data point in step 1.)
3. Make sure the Data Labels tab is selected.

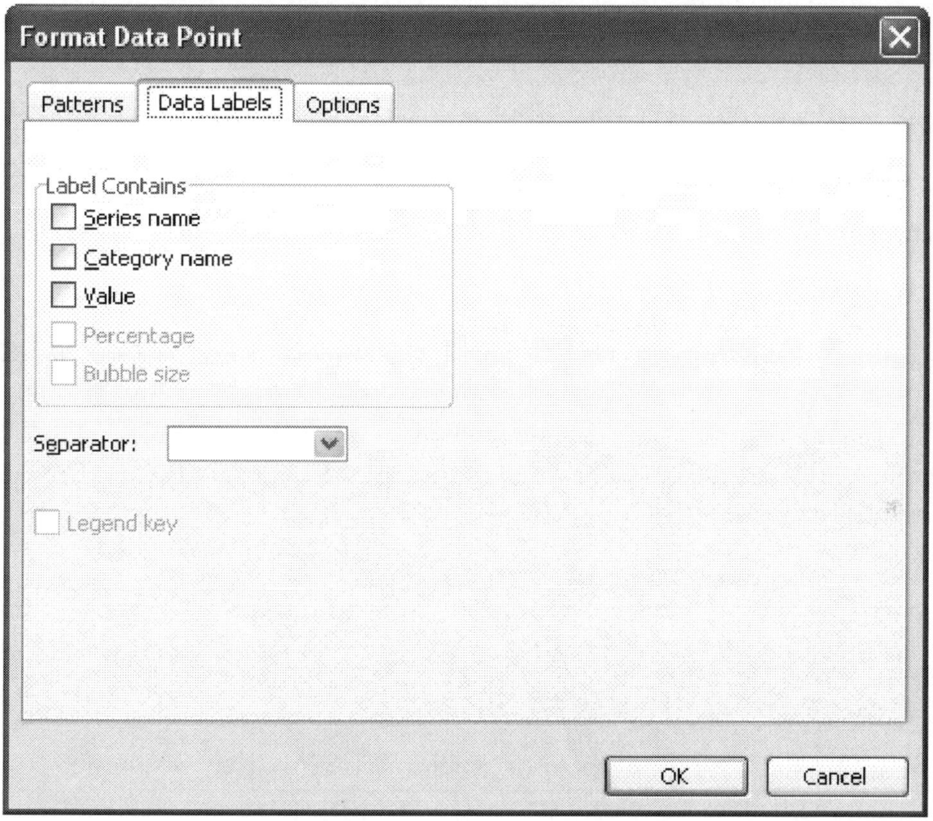

The Data Labels tab of the Format Data Point dialog box.

4. Make sure the Value check box is selected.
5. Click OK. The value of the data point appears, as a number, on the chart's representation of the data point.

6. Click the data label twice. (Don't double click; click once, wait a moment, then click again.) A small box should appear around the label.
7. In the Formula bar, enter the text you want used for the label. If desired, you can enter an equal sign followed by the call reference you want used for the label, as in =F7.
8. Click outside the data label; it should now appear as desired.

You can also format the data label's font and color, as desired, and you can move the data label's position by dragging it to a different area. The data label will maintain the same relative position to the data point, even when the chart is changed.

Moving Groups of Data Labels at One Time

Harry is looking for a way to select a group of data labels and move them, all in one operation. The problem is that Excel won't allow you to select and move a group of data labels, which means you need to adjust them individually.

Until such time as Microsoft decides to make working with chart labels more flexible, the best solution is to get a free Excel add-in called XY Chart Labeler, written by Rob Bovey. You can find the utility here:

```
http://appspro.com/Utilities/ChartLabeler.htm
```

Formatting Axis Patterns

Most people who create charts with Excel don't know that you can change just about everything that controls how the chart appears. One of the things you can easily change is the pattern used to denote a chart's axis. By default Excel normally uses a solid line for an axis. If you want to change the pattern used by Excel, follow these steps:

1. Right-click on the axis whose pattern you want to change. Excel displays a Context menu for the axis.
2. Choose Format Axis from the Context menu. (If there is no Format Axis choice, then you did not right-click on an axis in step 1.) Excel displays the Format Axis dialog box.
3. Make sure the Patterns tab is selected.

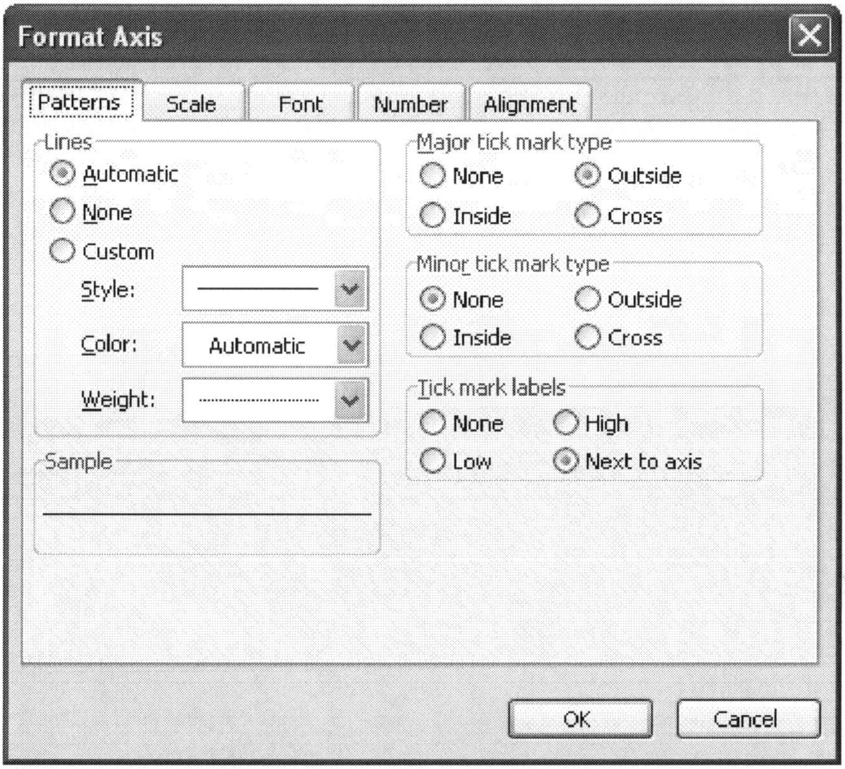

The Patterns tab of the Format Axis dialog box.

4. Use the Style drop-down list to select the pattern that Excel should use for the axis.
5. Use the Color drop-down list to select a color for the axis.

6. Use the Weight drop-down list to specify how dark the pattern should appear.
7. Click on OK.

Changing Axis Tick Marks

If you use an Excel chart type that uses axes, you may have noticed the presence of "tick marks" on one or all of the axes. Tick marks are used to indicate a major or minor demarcation along an axis. For instance, if you have an axis that ranges from 0 to 1000, there may be major tick marks at every 100 in the range, and minor tick marks at every 50.

Excel normally sets up the tick marks for you, but you can change the way they appear by following these steps:

1. Right-click on the axis whose tick marks you want to change. Excel displays a Context menu for the axis.
2. Choose Format Axis from the Context menu. (If there is no Format Axis choice, then you did not right-click on an axis in step 1.) Excel displays the Format Axis dialog box.
3. Make sure the Scale tab is selected.

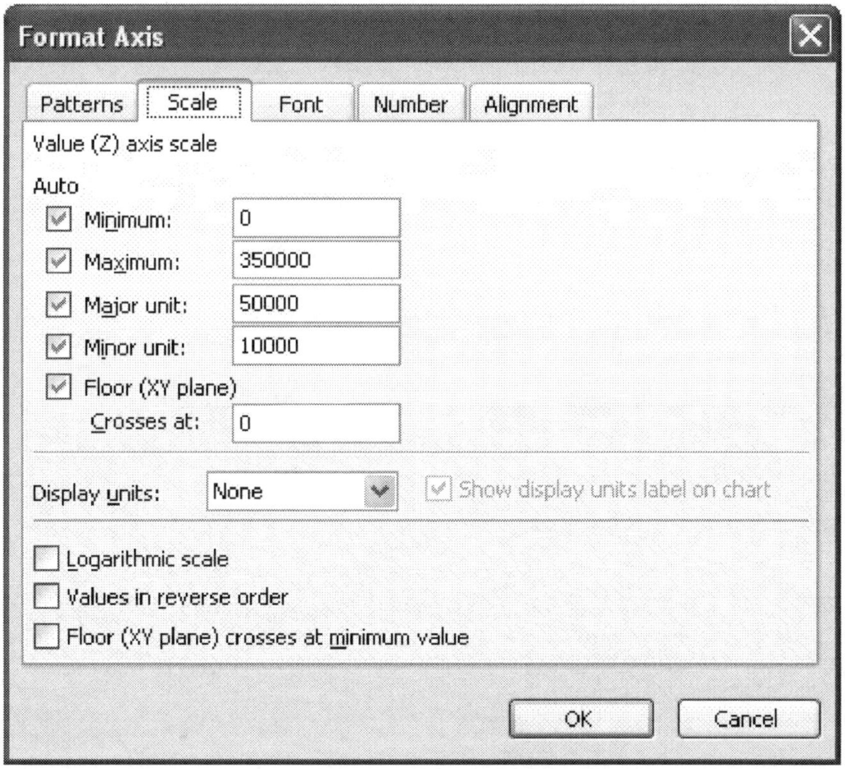

The Scale tab of the Format Axis dialog box.

4. Change the value to the right of Major Unit to indicate the multiple at which the major tick marks should appear.
5. Change the value to the right of Minor Unit to indicate the multiple at which the minor tick marks should appear.
6. Use the controls on the Scale tab to indicate where tick marks should appear along the axis.
7. Click on OK.

Changing the Axis Scale

Excel includes an impressive graphing capability that can turn the dullest data into outstanding charts, complete with all sorts of whiz-bang do-dads to amaze your friends and confound your enemies. While Excel can automatically handle many of the mundane tasks associated with turning raw data into a chart, you may still want to change some elements of your chart.

For instance, you may want to change the scale Excel uses along an axis of your chart. (The scale automatically chosen by Excel may not represent the entire universe of possibilities you want conveyed in your chart.) You can change the scale used by Excel by following these steps:

1. Right-click on the axis whose scale you want to change. Excel displays a Context menu for the axis.
2. Choose Format Axis from the Context menu. (If there is no Format Axis choice, then you did not right-click on an axis in step 1.) Excel displays the Format Axis dialog box.
3. Make sure the Scale tab is selected.

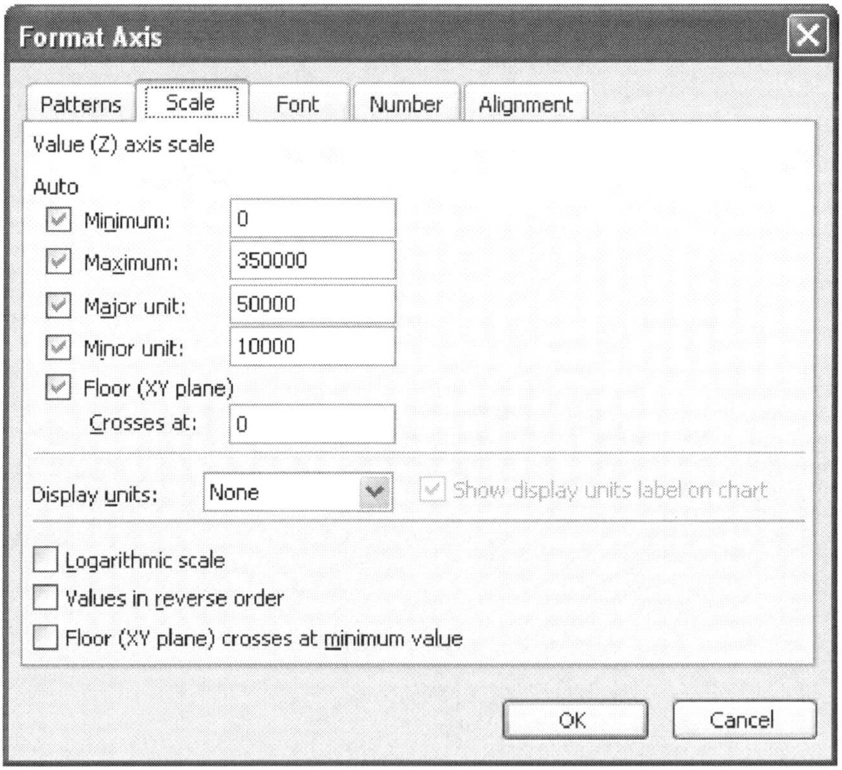

The Scale tab of the Format Axis dialog box.

4. Adjust the scale settings, as desired.
5. Click on OK.

Modifying Axis Scale Labels

It is very common for charts to use some sort of "shorthand" for values placed along an axis. For instance, if the values along an axis ranged from 0 to 80,000, you may want to have only the thousands portion of each value displayed on the axis. That way, instead of 20,000, 40,000, 60,000, and 80,000, you would see 20, 40, 60, and 80 along the axis. A note could then be made in a label that indicates the axis values are displayed in thousands.

You can very easily change the axis scale by simply modifying how the values on the axis are displayed. Follow these steps:

1. Create your chart as you normally would.
2. Double-click the axis you want to scale. You should see the Format Axis dialog box. (If double-clicking doesn't work, right-click the axis and choose Format Axis from the resulting Context menu.)
3. Make sure the Number tab is displayed.

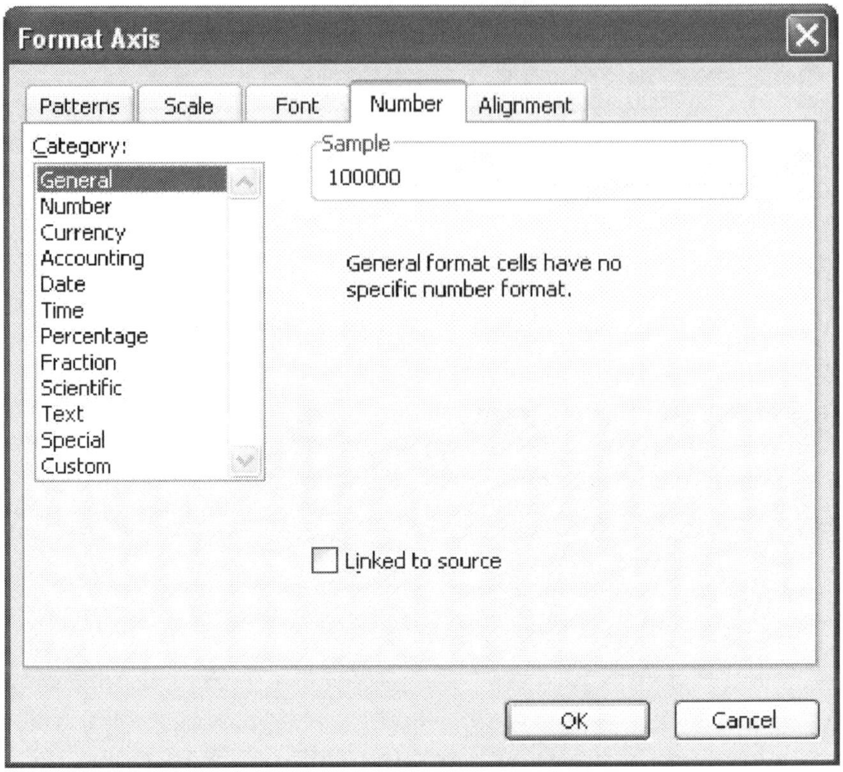

The Number tab of the Format Axis dialog box.

4. In the Category list, choose Custom.
5. In the Type box, enter a zero followed by a comma.
6. Click OK.

Only the thousands portion of the values in the axis should be displayed. You can then add another label, as desired, that indicates the values are expressed in thousands. If you'd prefer to not add the additional label, you can always use a format of "0,K" (without the quote marks) in step 5.

A different way to approach the problem is with these steps, which works in Excel 2000, Excel 2002, and Excel 2003:

1. Create your chart as you normally would.

2. Double-click the axis you want to scale. You should see the Format Axis dialog box. (If double-clicking doesn't work, right-click the axis and choose Format Axis from the resulting Context menu.)
3. Make sure the Scale tab is displayed.

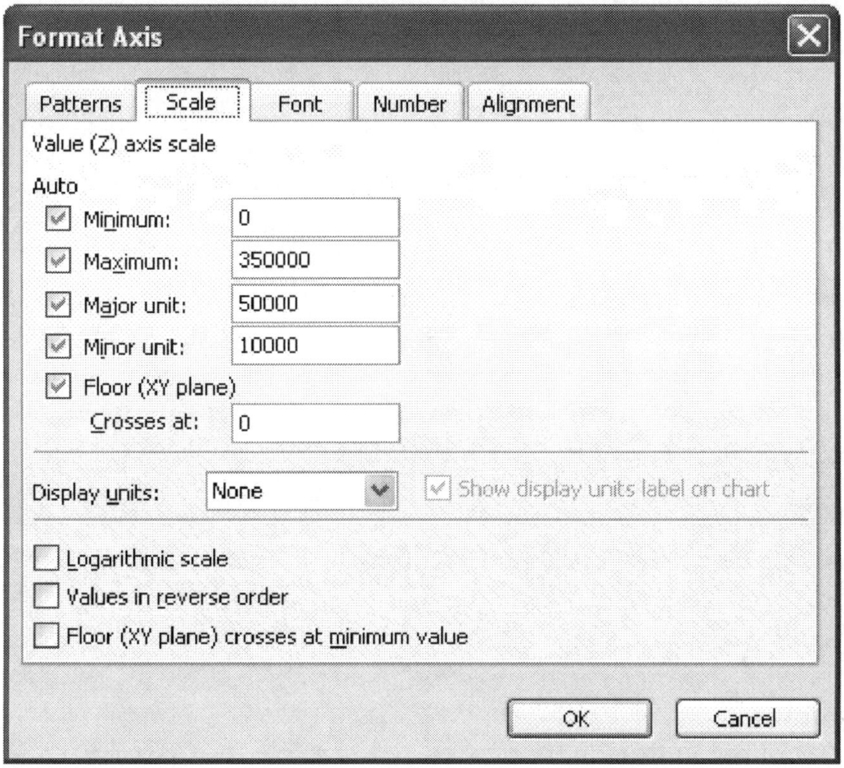

The Scale tab of the Format Axis dialog box.

4. Using the Display Units drop-down list, choose Thousands.
5. Click OK.

Excel changes the axis values so only the thousands portion is displayed, and inserts a label saying Thousands. Double-click on the Thousands label to edit the label, as desired, then drag it to any desired position.

Y-Axis Chart Titles are Truncated

Hao is running into a problem where his Y-axis titles are having the last 4 or 5 characters truncated, seemingly without rhyme or reason. In his case, the problem seems to be related somehow to the Analysis ToolPak, since the truncation doesn't occur until it is installed. Since he can't disable the Analysis ToolPak (he needs it to complete his calculations), Hao is wondering if others have run into the same problem and how they fixed it.

It seems that you're not the only one who has run into the problem, nor are you the only one who would love a solution. There doesn't seem to be a solution right now, but several subscribers provided workarounds that they use.

One possible workaround is to simply "pad" the end of the Y-axis title so that it contains inconsequential characters you don't mind having chopped off. For instance, you could add a few spaces at the end of the title, followed by a period. Or, you could try non-breaking spaces (without the period) by pressing **Ctrl+Shift+Space Bar**. If you pad the title with printable characters, you can format those characters so that they are the same color as the background.

It appears that the space allotted for the axis title by Excel is proportional to the size of the chart itself. This means that you may need to play with the chart size and see if enlarging it allows more of the axis title to be displayed. Some subscribers also reported success by adjusting the font size used for the axis title. For font sizes up to 26 or 28 points, the title would display correctly on a single line, but again this depended on the size of the chart itself.

Some people also got good results by adding a few spaces at the beginning of the axis title text. (Yes, at the beginning.) Why this works is unclear, other than it may force Excel to act as if there are spaces at the end, even though you didn't add any, in order to center the text in the available title space.

Two-Level Axis Labels

Excel is great at creating charts. With some types of data, you may have a need for two-level axis labels for your chart. For instance, you may want something similar to the following along the X-axis for your chart:

```
Pro | Team | Reg | Pro | Team | Reg ...
  Eastern US     |   Western US ...
```

Setting up such an arrangement in an Excel worksheet is easy, but getting the same result in a chart may not be as obvious.

Go ahead and set up your worksheet to reflect the column titles the way you want them. These column titles will end up as your X-axis labels. You could set them up as follows:

```
  |   A   |   B   |   C   |   D   |   E   |   F   |   G   |
1 |       |      Eastern US       |      Western US       |
2 |       |  Pro  | Team  |  Reg  |  Pro  | Team  |  Reg  |
```

1. In the first row, put your first major group title into cell B1.
2. Put your second major group title into cell E1.
3. In cells B2:G2 place your column labels.
4. Select cells B1:D1 and click the Merge and Center tool. The first major group title should now be centered over the first group of column labels.
5. Select cells E1:G1 and click the Merge and Center tool. The second major group title should now be centered over the second group of column labels.
6. Make the cells at B1:G2 bold. (This sets them off from your data.)
7. Place your row labels into column A, beginning at cell A3.
8. Place your data into the table, beginning at cell B3.

With your table completed, you are ready to create the chart. Just select your data table, including all the headings in the first two rows, then create your chart. Excel automatically recognizes that you have two rows being used for the X-axis labels, and formats the chart correctly. Since the X-axis labels appear beneath the chart data, the order of the label rows is reversed—exactly as mentioned at the first of this tip.

	Eastern US			Western US		
	Pro	Team	Reg	Pro	Team	Reg
Harris	1	2	3	2	3	4
Brown	4	5	6	7	5	6
Jones	7	8	9	5	6	8

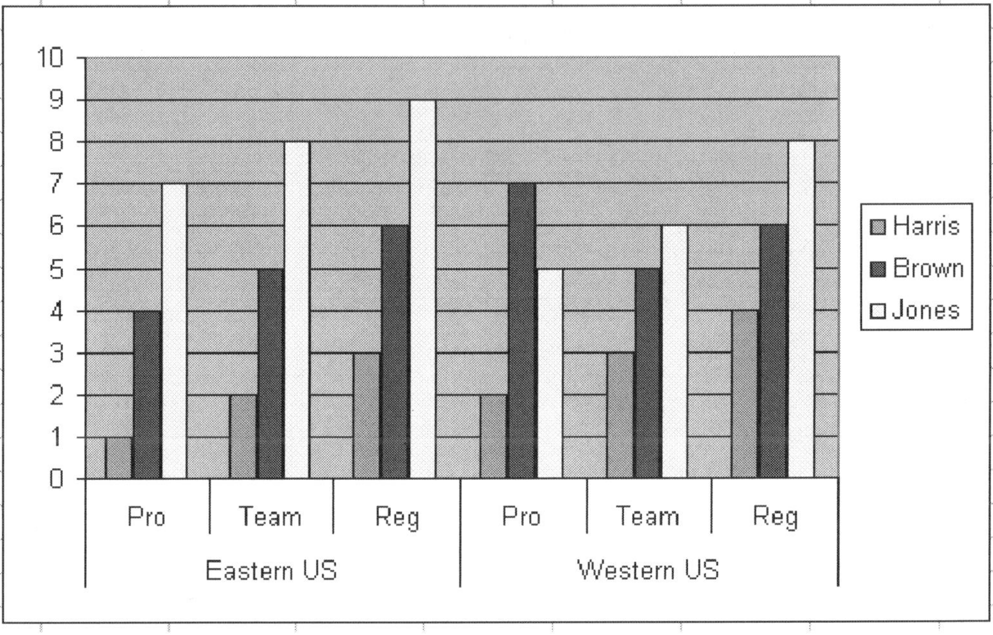

Two-level axis labels are created automatically by Excel.

Numeric Value and Percentage Value in a Graph Column

Harrie wants to create a column chart that displays two values for each column in the chart. One value to be displayed would be a percentage (such as 46%) and the other an absolute value (such as 359,000). One value would appear on the column in the chart, and the other just above the column.

There are many ways that this can be accomplished, depending on the nature of your data. This tip will examine a couple of the many ways you can proceed.

A relatively simple approach is to assume that your data is in three columns. The first column is the category (what will appear along the X-axis), the second is the percentage that you want to plot, and the third is the absolute value to be displayed. Follow these steps:

1. Select all three columns of data and start the Chart Wizard. (Click the Chart Wizard toolbar button.)
2. In the first step of the wizard, choose a Column chart type, with a Clustered Column sub-type.
3. Click Finish. You now have a simple chart displaying the percentage on the Y-axis. There are, however, two sets of Y-coordinate data that are plotted.
4. On the chart, double-click the second series (the "exact amount" values). Excel displays the Patterns tab of the Format Data Series dialog box.

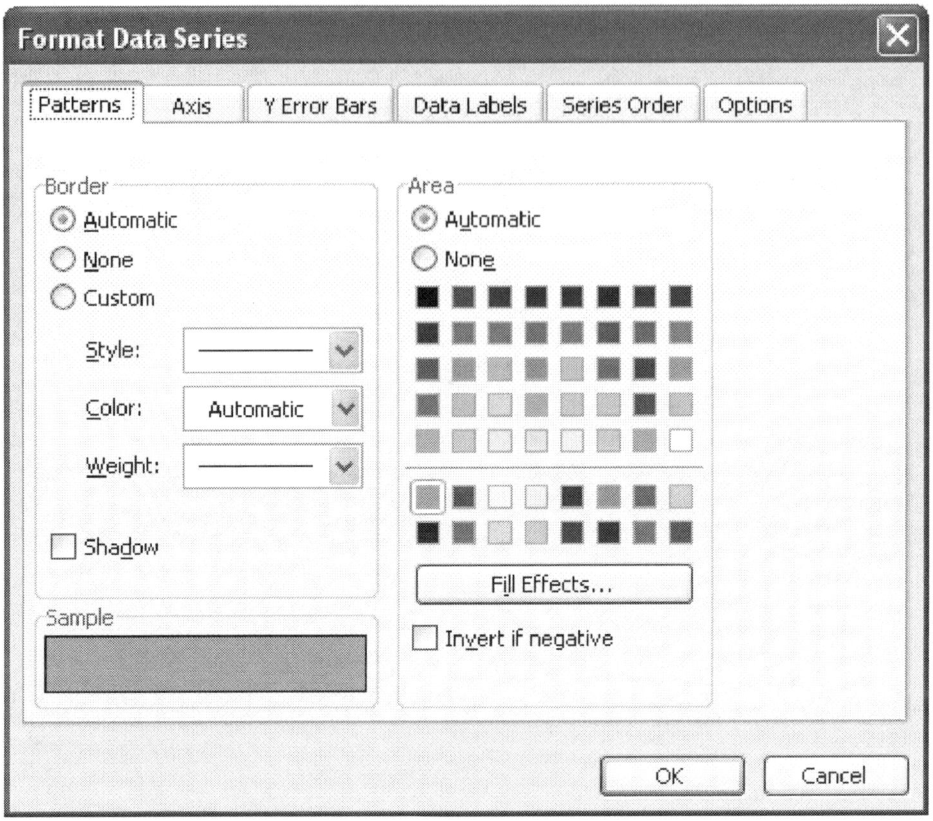

The Patterns tab of the Format Data Series dialog box.

5. Click the None option buttons in both the Border and Area portions of the dialog box.
6. Display the Axis tab.
7. Click the Second Axis option button.
8. Display the Data Labels tab.
9. Select the Value (or Show Values) check box.
10. Click OK. You now have the absolute values displayed, yet you've hidden the graph column in which they would normally be displayed.
11. Double-click the second Y-axis (the one on the right). Excel displays the Patterns tab of the Format Axis dialog box.

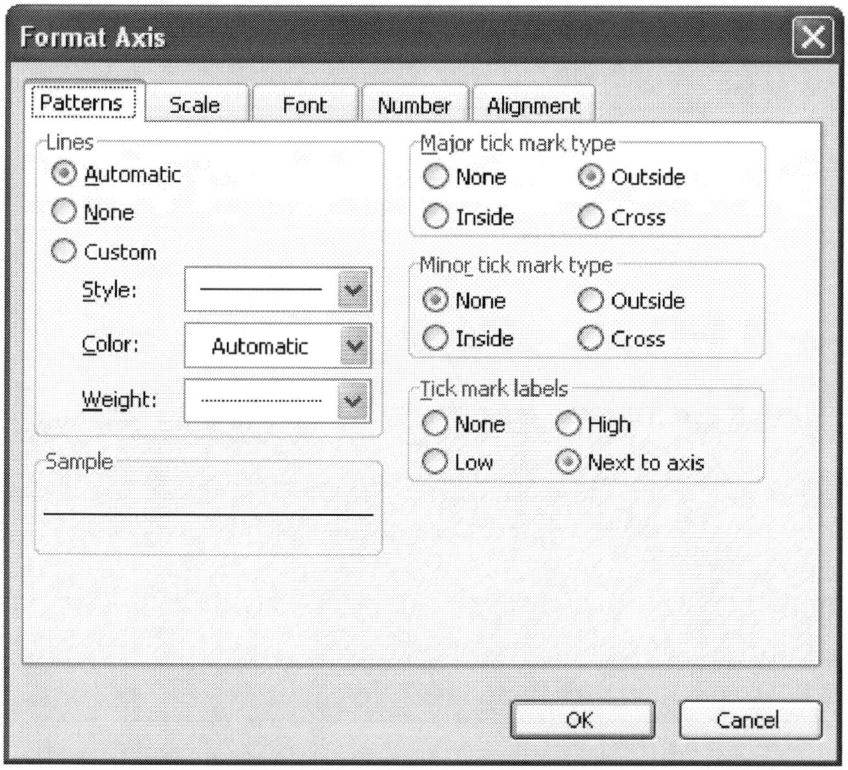

The Patterns tab of the Format Axis dialog box.

12. Make sure that all the None option buttons on the dialog are chosen.
13. Click OK. The secondary axis should now be gone from the graph.
14. Double-click one of the data labels (the absolute values). Excel displays the Format Data Labels dialog box.
15. On the Alignment tab, change the Label Position drop-down list to Center.
16. Click OK. The data labels should now be centered within each column.
17. Double-click the remaining data series (the percentage values). Excel displays the Patterns tab of the Format Data Series dialog box.
18. Display the Data Labels tab.
19. Select the Value (or Show Values) check box.
20. Click OK. The percentage value should now appear above each column.

Plotting Times of Day

Richard has some source data that shows the date and time displayed in the format dd/mm/yy hh:mm, but when he creates a chart from that data, the only thing that is plotted is the date. He is wondering if there is a way of plotting the times on the chart, as well as the date.

There are several ways you can approach this issue, depending on the type of chart you want to create. If you create an X-Y scatter chart, the date and time should plot automatically. This is not the case if you choose to create a bar, column line, or any other type of chart. In those cases, the X axis is created from equally spaced values, so you won't get exactly what you want.

If you don't want to use a scatter chart, then you could simply modify the data in your source. Add a column that represents the hour of the day, derived through the HOUR function. For instance, if you have your date and time in column B, add a column C and fill it with formulas such as =HOUR(B3). The result is a bunch of numbers representing the hour of the day, 0 through 23. This can chart very easily in any manner desired.

If that doesn't fit your needs, then go ahead and create the chart as you normally would. Then, right-click the X axis and choose Format Axis from the Context menu. You should see the Format Axis dialog box. Make sure the Number tab is selected.

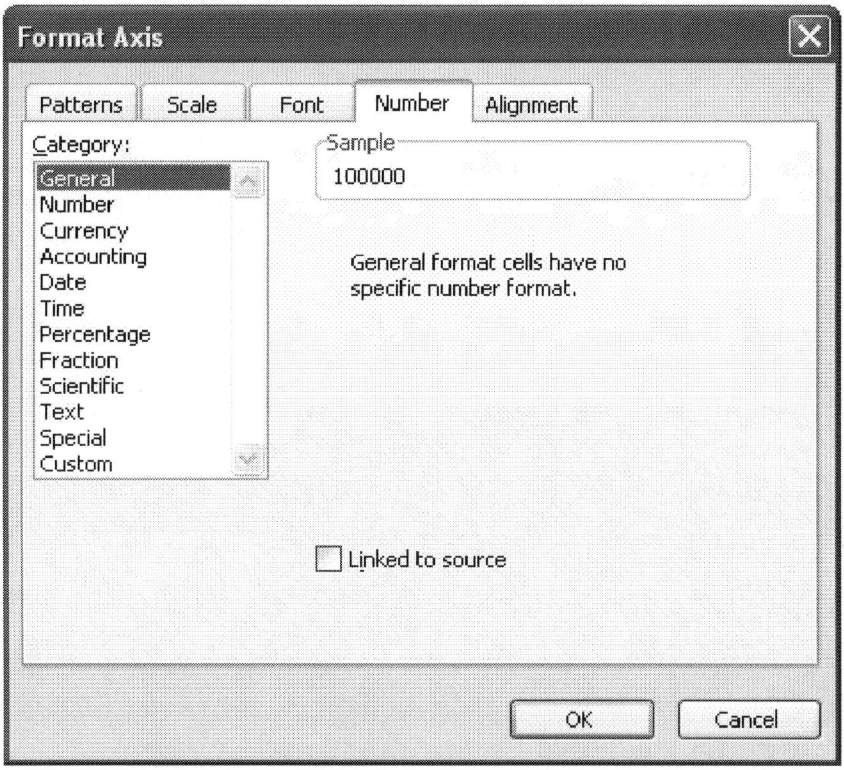

The Number tab of the Format Axis dialog box.

Choose one of the formats for the axis under either the Date or Time categories. You may have to play a bit with your selection, experimenting to find out what works best. Quite honestly, what works best in one situation won't necessarily work best in another because of the nature of the data being charted.

You can find more information about formatting time values on an axis at this Web site:

`http://www.mrexcel.com/articles/excel-time-series-chart.php`

Graphically Charting Geographic Data

Kauai has students from all over the country enrolled in classes at his school. He would like to build a graphical chart of the US states, charting our enrollments by state and color code the states based on the number of enrollments from that state.

In Excel 97 and Excel 2000 there is a built-in "mapping" feature that you can use to create the desired map. The feature was removed in Excel 2002 and made into a separate product called Microsoft MapPoint. If you have Excel 97 or Excel 2000, you can learn how to use the feature by referring to this page in the Microsoft Knowledge Base:

```
http://support.microsoft.com/?kbid=147637
```

If you are using a later version of Excel, then you won't be able to create the desired map with Excel; you will need to get an additional program, such as Microsoft MapPoint (http://www.microsoft.com/mappoint) or SPSS (http://www.spss.com). (Creating the desired map with SPSS is very easy to do.)

If you want something a little more complex than a simple color graphic, you could use a free program to map the data, such as Google Earth (http://earth.google.com). You can export your student's data from Excel to a simple CSV file, and then import it into Google Earth so that the individual student locations can be superimposed over a satellite map.

Adjusting Your View of 3-D Graphs

Excel allows you to create some great looking three-dimensional graphs based on the information in your worksheets. For many purposes, the default method in which the graphs are created will be sufficient for your needs. However, you may want to adjust the angle at which you view your graph. Excel makes this easy by following these steps:

1. Create and display your 3-D graph as you normally would.
2. Select the 3-D View option from the Chart menu. Excel displays the 3-D View dialog box.

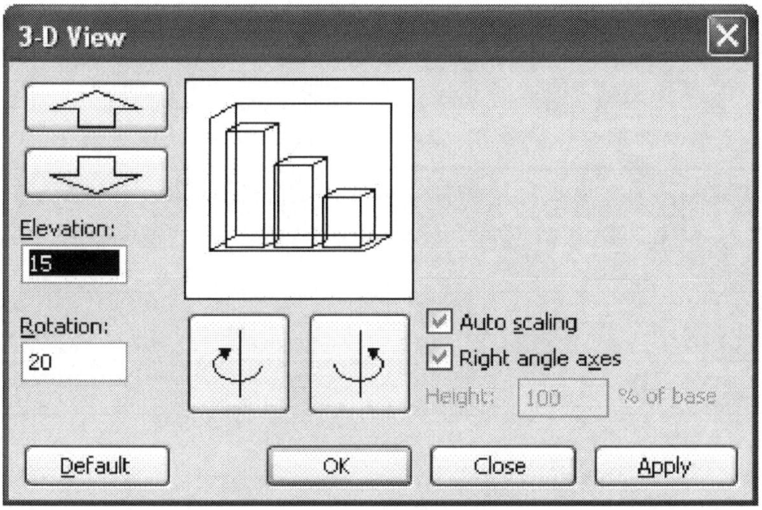

The 3-D View dialog box.

3. Using the appropriate boxes, specify an elevation, rotation, and perspective that are desired. You can also use the buttons to adjust the values in the boxes. As you make changes, Excel displays a frame outline of how a 3-D graph appears.
4. When satisfied, click on OK. Your graph is updated with the adjusted view.

Using the Mouse to Adjust Your View of 3-D Graphs

When you create a 3-D graph with Excel, you might want to adjust the perspective of the graph just a bit. You can use dialog boxes to make the adjustment, but you don't need to go to that trouble—you can use the mouse. All you need to do is follow these steps:

1. Create and display your 3-D graph as you normally would.
2. Click on the walls that define the sides of your 3-D graph. Don't click on the objects that represent the data, but on the walls surrounding the data. A good place to click is on the gray back walls of the graph.

3. Move the mouse pointer over the corners of the graph, where some of the small graphic handles (small black boxes) appear. When you do, a ToolTip should appear that says "Corners."
4. Click on the corner. This selects the corner.
5. Click again on the corner, but don't release the mouse button. Instead, start to drag the corner in the direction you want.

When you perform step 5, Excel erases the graph and displays an outline of the box that contains the graph. You can drag the corner any direction you want, and Excel adjusts the angle at which you view the box. When you release the mouse button, the graph is redrawn at the current viewing angle.

Exploded Pie Chart Sections

Gloria asked if there was a way, in a 3-D pie chart, to "explode" groups of slices, instead of individual slices. When you pick an exploded pie chart as your chart type, all the slices of the pie are "pushed back," away from the center of the pie. Gloria was looking for a way to have different slices grouped together in the view.

There is no way to group individual slices of the pie prior to exploding, nor does Excel provide a way to push selected slices together. There are, however, a couple of workarounds that can be tried.

The first approach is to make a chart for every grouping in your original data. Each chart is based on the entire original data table, but you set the colors for the group to be represented by the particular chart, and then make the other groups "invisible" by turning off their borders and colors. You can then overlay the charts to get the desired effect. This approach obviously would require some experimentation to get exactly the right look, but it is a great approach if the data that underlies the table will change periodically.

Another approach is to treat your pie chart as a drawing object. This gives you a great deal of flexibility, and is most appropriate for "one up" charts that won't be later changed. Follow these general steps:

1. Create an exploded pie chart based on your data, formatting the chart as desired. (Each slice should be exploded.)
2. Select the chart by clicking on it.
3. Hold down the **Shift** key as you select the Edit menu. (This affects the choices shown in the menu.)
4. Choose Copy Picture from the menu. Excel displays the Copy Picture dialog box.

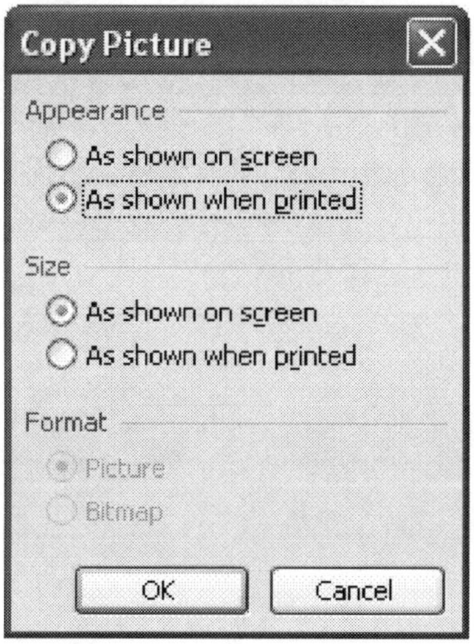

The Copy Picture dialog box.

5. Make sure the As Shown When Printed option is selected, then click on OK. The picture is now on the Clipboard.
6. Display a blank worksheet.
7. Press **Ctrl+V**. The chart is now displayed as a picture in the worksheet.
8. Right-click on the picture. Excel displays a Context menu for the image.
9. Choose Grouping, then Ungroup. Excel asks if you want to convert the picture to a Microsoft Office drawing object.
10. Click on Yes. The image is converted, and every item in the chart is now selected.
11. Individually select and delete any items you don't want kept.

12. Select and move the various parts of the pie chart, as desired. (Excel considers each panel of a 3-D slice to be an object. Thus, if you want to move a slice, you need to select the top and sides and move them together.)

Deleting a Chart

Excel allows you to create all sorts of charts based on the data in a worksheet table. These charts can either be on their own sheets or they can be embedded within a regular worksheet. At some point you may have a need to delete a chart. To delete an embedded chart, all you need to do is select it (so that handles appear around the perimeter of the chart object) and then press the **DELETE** key. If you need to delete a chart sheet, you do so in the same manner as when you delete a regular worksheet:

1. Display the chart sheet.
2. Choose Delete Sheet from the Edit menu. Excel asks if you are sure you want to delete the sheet.
3. Click on OK. The chart sheet is deleted.

13

Working with Chart Data

Excluding Some Data from a Chart

Pam keeps a month's worth of data in a table and created a chart based on that data. The data was collected from information generated on her company's shop floor. The data includes weekends, but Pam doesn't want the weekend data included in the chart. She knows that she could hide the rows and they would be excluded from the chart, but she still needs the hidden rows to be displayed in the table. In other words, she wants them displayed in the data table, but not in the chart.

There are a couple of ways you could approach this problem. One is to simply make a copy of your data (maybe copy the whole worksheet) and then delete the rows that contain weekend data. You would still have your master data for whatever purposes you need, but you could base your chart on the modified copy of that data.

The drawback to this, of course, is that it creates two sets of data that may need to be updated or kept in sync in some way. It may be better to base your chart on a non-contiguous data range. Assume, for a moment, that your data was in A1:B15, and that there were weekends in rows 7, 8, 14, and 15. You could, within the chart, set the data range for the source data to this:

```
=Sheet1!$A$1:$B$6,Sheet1!$A$9:$B$13
```

You could also create a named range that refers to the non-contiguous ranges you want included in the chart. You could then use the named range in your chart, as a reference to the source data.

Finally, if you don't mind adding another column to your data, you could use the new column for your chart source. Assume, for a moment, that your readings are in column A and the dates of those readings are in column B. In each cell of column C you could place the following formula:

```
=IF(WEEKDAY(B1,2)>5,NA(),A1)
```

You then end up with a series of readings for all weekdays; the weekends show #N/A for the reading. You can base your chart on this data and Excel will ignore the #N/A values. You can even hide column C so it does not distract from your source data.

Dynamic Data Based on Chart Changes

Ben knows how to create a chart based on data in a worksheet. If he later changes the data on which the chart is based, Excel will update the chart to reflect the change. He wonders, however, if there is a way, perhaps with an add-on, that he can drag points in his chart and have those changes reflect back into the data.

This is a feature that is already built into Excel; no extra add-on is necessary. If you create a chart, click on a single data point, and then hover the mouse over the data point, you'll see that it changes to a double-headed arrow. Once this happens, drag the data point as you desire. When you release the mouse button, the data upon which the chart is based is modified to reflect the new position of the data point.

Automatically Creating Charts for Individual Rows in a Data Table

David has a worksheet that he uses to track sales by company over a number of months. The company names are in column A and up to fifteen months of sales are in columns B:P. David would like to create a chart that could be dynamically changed to show the sales for a single company from the worksheet.

There are several ways that this can be done; I'll examine three of them in this tip. For the sake of example, let's assume that the worksheet is named MyData, and that the first row contains data headers. The company names are in the range A2:A151, and the sales data for those companies is in B2:P151.

One approach is to use Excel's AutoFilter capabilities. Create your chart as you normally would, making sure that the chart is configured to draw its data series from the rows of the MyData worksheet. You should also place the chart on its own sheet.

Now, select A1 on MyData and apply an AutoFilter (Data | Filter | AutoFilter). A small drop-down arrow appears at the top of each column. Click the drop-down arrow for column A and select the company you want to view in the chart. Excel redraws the chart to include only the single company.

The only potential drawback to the AutoFilter approach is that each company is considered an independent data series, even though only one of them is displayed in the chart. Because they are independent, each company is charted in a different color. If you want the same charting colors to always be used, then you will need to use one of the other approaches.

Another way to approach the problem is through the use of an "intermediate" data table—one that is created dynamically, pulling only the information you want from the larger data table. The chart is then based on the dynamic intermediate table. Follow these steps:

1. Create a new worksheet and name it something like "ChartData".
2. Copy the column headers from the MyData worksheet to the second row on the ChartData sheet. (In other words, copy MyData!A1:P1 to ChartData!A2:P2. This leaves the first row of the ChartData sheet temporarily empty.)
3. With the MyData worksheet displayed, choose View | Toolbars | Forms. The Forms toolbar should be displayed.

4. Using the Forms toolbar, draw a Combo Box control somewhere on the MyData worksheet.
5. Display the Format Control dialog box for the newly created Combo Box. (Right-click the Combo Box and choose Format Control.)
6. Using the controls in the dialog box, specify the Input Range as MyData!$A$2:$A$151, specify the Cell Link as ChartData!$A$1, and specify the Drop Down Lines as 25 (or whatever figure you want).

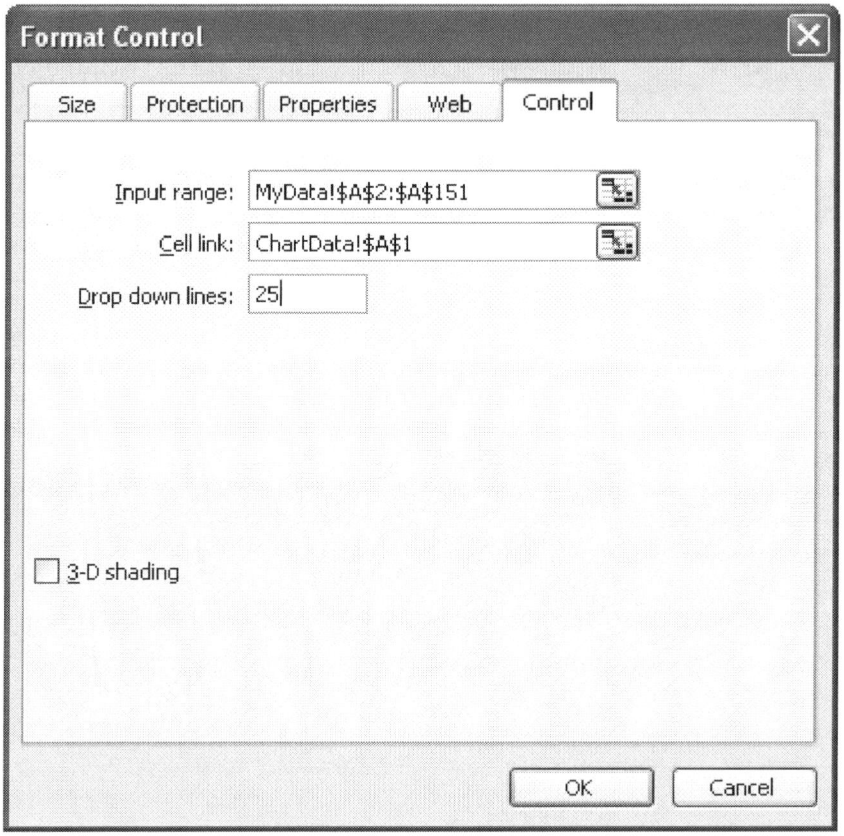

The Format Control dialog box.

7. Click OK to dismiss the dialog box. You now have a functioning Combo Box that, once you use it to select a company name, will place a value in cell A1 of the ChartData worksheet that indicates what you selected.

8. With the ChartData worksheet displayed, enter the following formula into cell A3:

```
=INDEX(MyData!A2:A151,$A$1)
```

9. Copy the contents of cell A3 to the range B3:P3. Row 3 now contains the data of whatever company is selected in the Combo Box.

10. In cell B1 enter the following formula. (The result of this formula will act as the title for your dynamic chart.)

```
="Data for " & A3
```

11. Select the column headers and data (B2:P3) and create a chart based on this data. Set the chart's title to some placeholder text; it doesn't matter what it is right now.

12. In the finished chart, select the chart title.

13. In the Formula bar, enter the following formula:

```
=ChartData!$A$3
```

You now have a fully functioning dynamic chart. You can use the Combo Box to select a different company, and the chart is redrawn using the data for the company you select. If you want, you can move or copy the Combo Box to the sheet containing your chart so that you can view the updated chart every time you make a selection. You can also, if desired, hide the ChartData worksheet.

A third approach is to use a macro to modify the range on which a chart is based. To prepare for this approach, create two named ranges in your workbook. The first name should be ChartTitle, and it should refer to the formula =OFFSET(MyData!$A$1,22,0,1,1) Click Add, and then define the second name. This one should be called ChartXRange, and it should refer to the formula =OFFSET(MyData!$A$1,22,0,1,15).

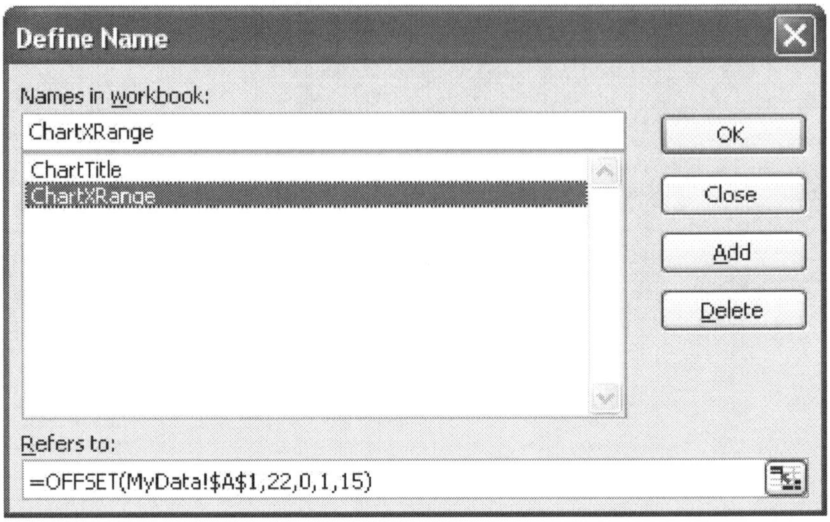

The Define Name dialog box.

With the names defined, you can select the range MyData!B1:P2 and create your chart. You should base the chart on this simple range, and make sure that you place some temporary text in the chart title. Make sure the chart is created on its own sheet and that you name the sheet ChartSheet.

With the chart created, right-click the chart and choose Source Data. Excel displays the Source Data dialog box, and you should choose the Series tab. Since you based the chart on the headers and a single row of data, there should be a single data series in the dialog box. Replace whatever is in the Values box with the following formula:

```
='Book1'!ChartXRange
```

Make sure you replace Book1 with the name of the workbook in which you are working. Click OK, and the chart is now based on the named range you specified earlier. You can now select the chart title and place the following in the Formula bar to make the title dynamic:

```
=MyData!ChartTitle
```

Now you are ready to add the macro that makes everything dynamic. Display the VBA Editor and add the following macro to the code window for the

MyData worksheet. (Double-click the worksheet name in the Project Explorer area.)

```
Private Sub Worksheet_BeforeDoubleClick(ByVal Target As Excel.Range, Cancel
As Boolean)
    ActiveWorkbook.Names.Add Name:="ChartXRange", _
        RefersToR1C1:="=OFFSET(MyData!R1C1," & _
            ActiveCell.Row - 1 & ",1,1,15)"
    ActiveWorkbook.Names.Add Name:="ChartTitle", _
        RefersToR1C1:="=OFFSET(MyData!R1C1," & _
            ActiveCell.Row - 1 & ",0,1,1)"
    Sheets("ChartSheet").Activate
    Cancel = True
End Sub
```

Now you can display the MyData worksheet and double-click any row. (Well, double-click in column A for a row.) The macro then updates the named ranges so that they point to the row on which you double-clicked, and then displays the ChartSheet sheet. The chart (and title) are redrawn to reflect the data in the row on which you double-clicked.

Smoothing Out Data Series

When you are creating line charts in Excel, the lines drawn between data points tend to be very straight. (This makes sense; the lines are meant to connect the points.) You can give your graphs a more professional look by simply smoothing out the curves Excel uses at each data point. Follow these steps:

1. In your chart, right-click on the data series that you want to smooth. Excel displays a Context menu.
2. Choose Format Data Series from the Context menu. Excel displays the Format Data Series dialog box.
3. Make sure the Patterns tab is displayed.

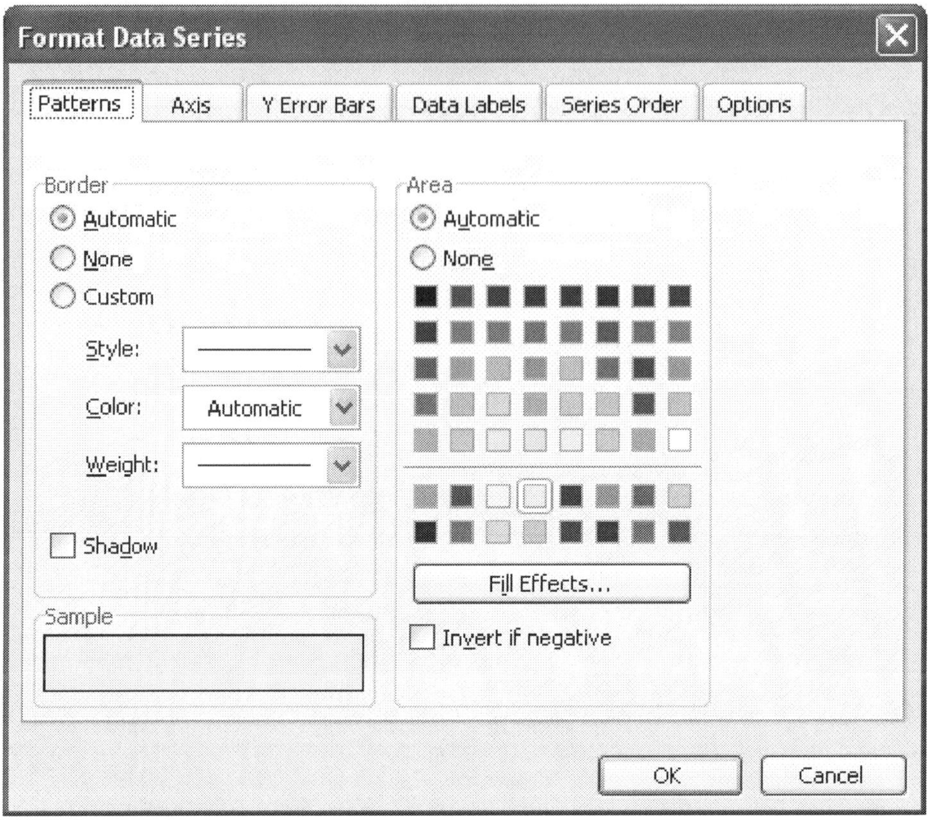

The Patterns tab of the Format Data Series dialog box.

4. Select the Smoothed Line check box.
5. Click on OK.

Changing the Pattern Used in a Data Series

When you create a chart with Excel, you typically use the Chart Wizard to create the chart basic, and then make changes to prepare the final chart exactly as you want it. One of the things that Excel allows you to control is the pattern used to fill the graphic representation of a data series.

Normally, series are presented as appropriate for the type of chart you are creating, and then filled with varying colors. For most charts this may be more than adequate. However, you may want to change the pattern used in a data series, instead of using the solid color used by default. To do this, follow these steps:

1. Create your chart as you normally would.
2. Click on the data series that you want to customize. There should be selection handles that appear around the data series elements.
3. Choose Selected Data Series from the Format menu. Excel displays the Format Data Series dialog box.
4. Make sure the Patterns tab is selected.

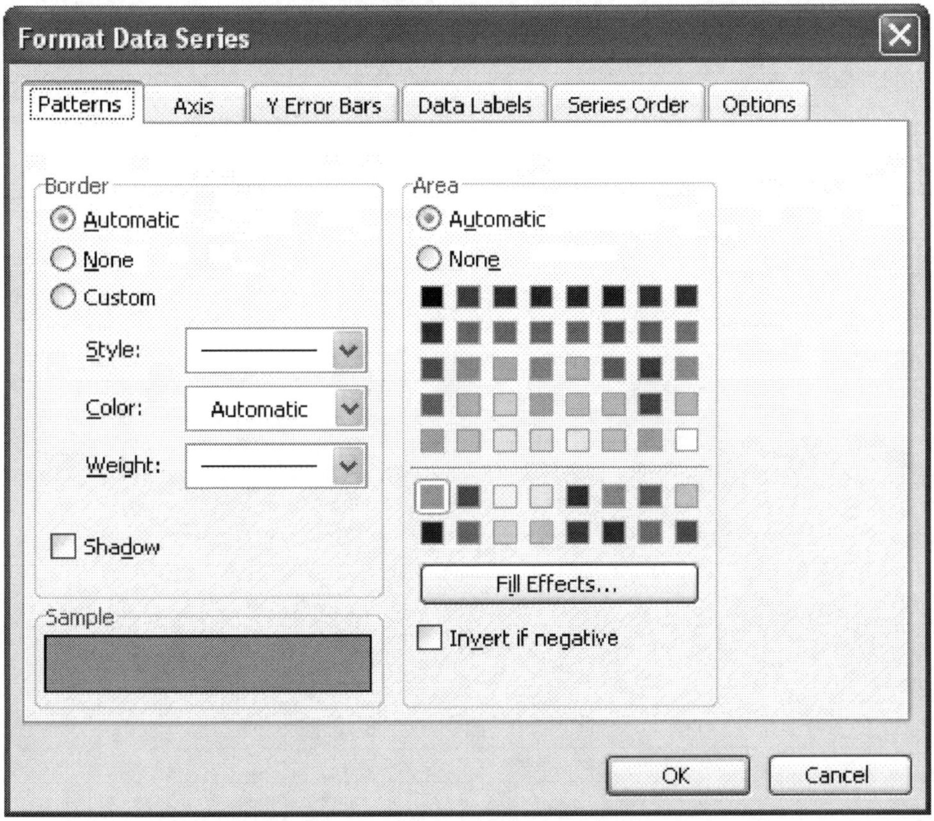

The Patterns tab of the Format Data Series dialog box.

5. Click on the Fill Effects button. Excel displays the Fill Effects dialog box.
6. Make sure the Pattern tab is selected.

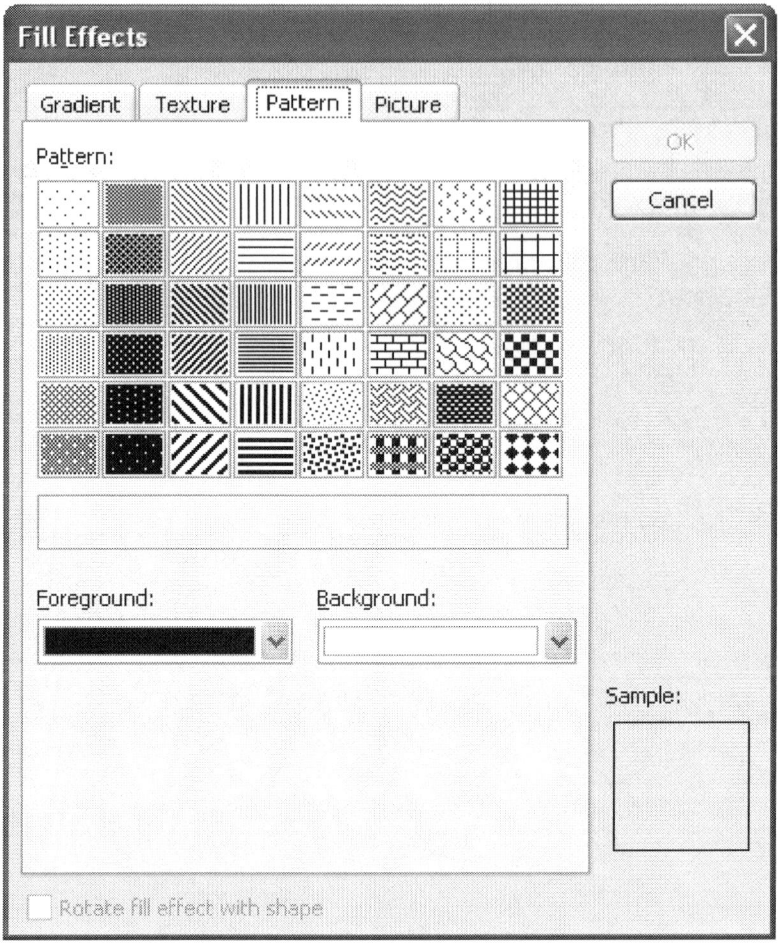

The Pattern tab of the Fill Effects dialog box.

7. From the selections in the dialog box, choose the pattern you want applied to the data series.
8. Click on OK to close the Fill Effects dialog box.
9. Click on OK to close the Format Data Series dialog box.

Using Graphics to Represent Data Series

Excel is great at creating all sorts of charts from your data. You can even customize the charts to your heart's content. One of the customizations you can make is to replace the regular bars (in a bar chart) with your own graphics. For instance, you might have a small graphic of a house that you want to use for the bars. This could be great if you wanted to used "stacked" houses to represent, for instance, housing starts in an area.

To use your own graphics in place of Excel's built-in bars, follow these steps:

1. Create your bar chart as usual.
2. Right click on one of the data series bars in the chart. Excel displays a Context menu.
3. Choose Format Data Series from the Context menu. Excel displays the Format Data Series dialog box.
4. Make sure the Patterns tab is selected.

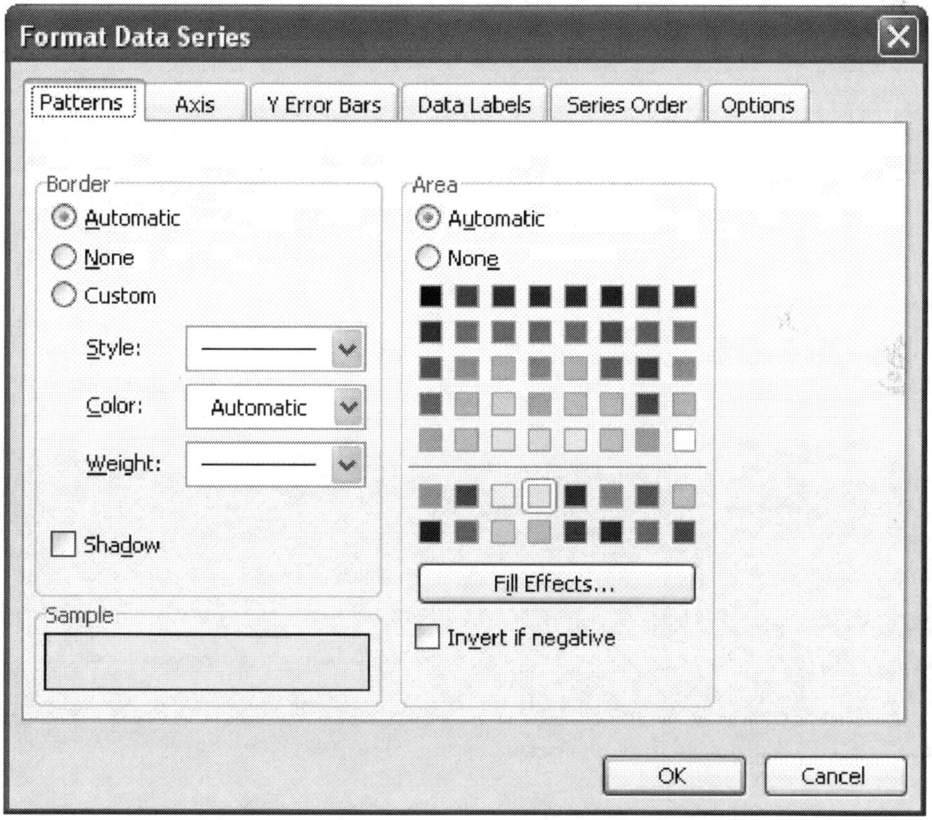

The Patterns tab of the Format Data Series dialog box.

5. Click on Fill Effects. Excel displays the Fill Effects dialog box.
6. Make sure the Picture tab is selected.

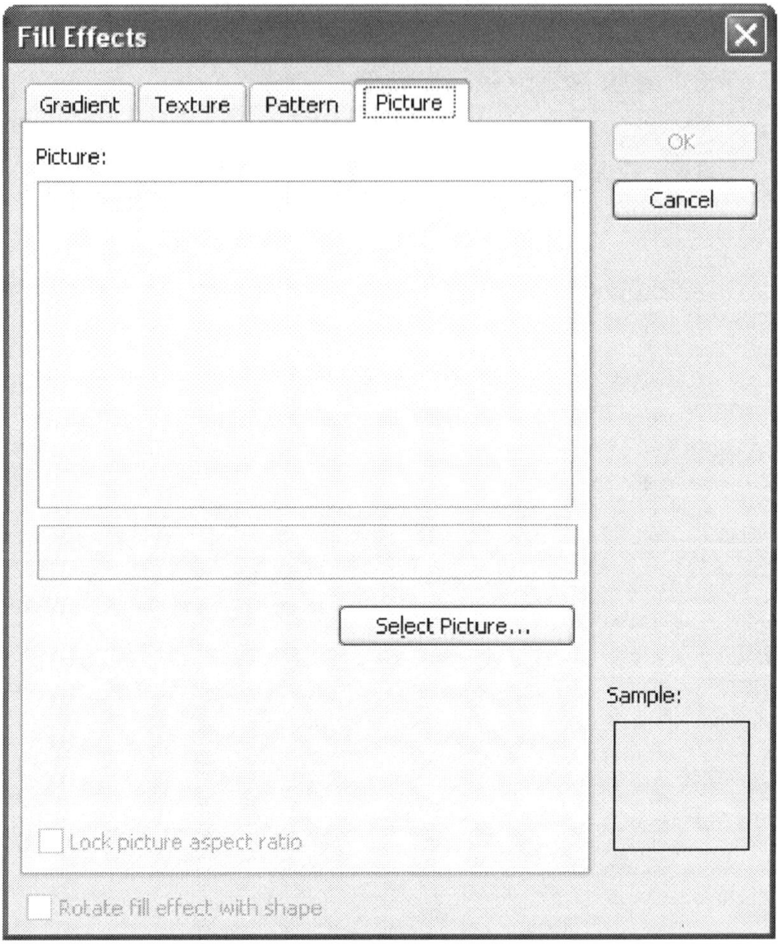

The Picture tab of the Fill Effects dialog box.

7. Click on Select Picture. Excel displays the Select Picture dialog box, which is very similar to a standard Open dialog box.
8. Use the controls in the dialog box to locate and select the picture you want to use.

9. Click on Insert. Excel closes the Select Picture dialog box and redisplays the Fill Effects dialog box.
10. In the Format section of the Picture tab, choose how you want the graphic to be applied to the bar. (I like to choose Stack And Scale To and then specify how to many units each picture represents.)
11. Click on OK in each open dialog box to close them.

Reordering the Display of a Data Series

When you create a chart in Excel, you may have a need to change the order in which the data series are displayed in the chart. One way to do this, of course, is to change the order of the data in the underlying worksheet range. For instance, you can sort the data in the worksheet range, and the change in order should be reflected in the chart based on that data.

Another way is to manually customize the chart to rearrange the data series. Follow these steps:

1. Right-click on one of the data series that you want to move. Excel displays a Context menu.
2. Select the Format Data Series option from the Context menu. Excel displays the Format Data Series dialog box.
3. Make sure the Series Order tab is displayed.

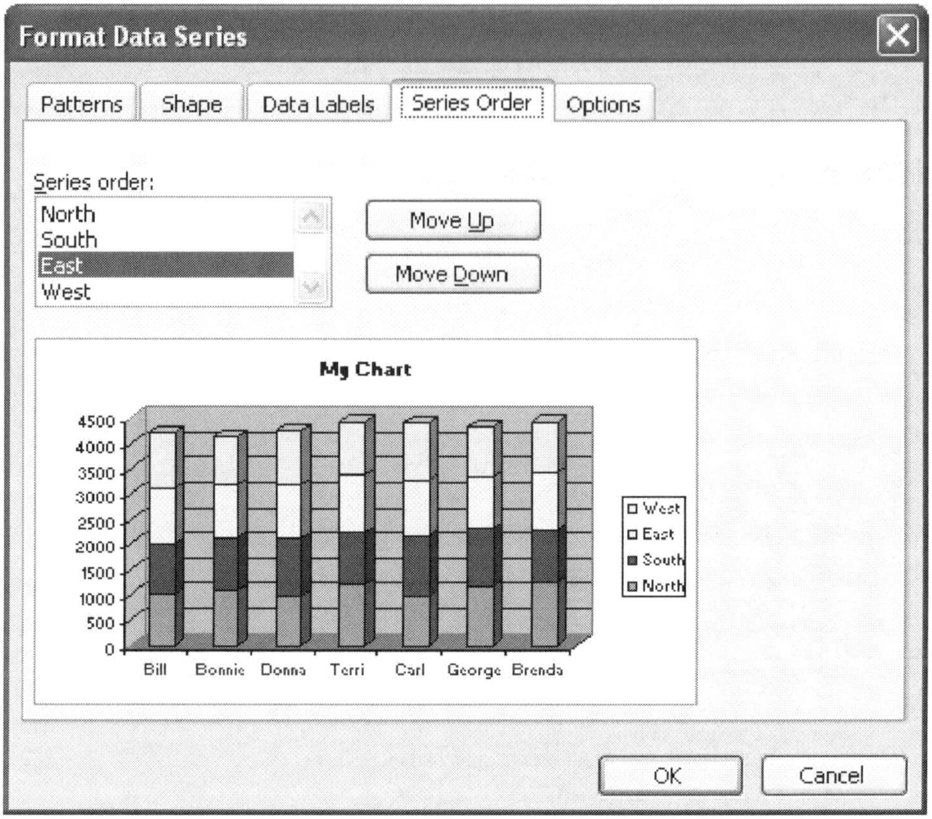

The Series Order tab of the Format Data Series dialog box.

4. Click on Move Up or Move Down to move the data series to a new relative location.
5. If desired, select another data series in the Series Order list and repeat step 4.
6. When finished, click on OK.

Easily Changing Chart Data Ranges

Excel is great when it comes to creating charts based on data in a data table. The Chart Wizard can quickly identify an entire data table, or you can select a portion of a data table and use the Chart Wizard to create a chart based just on that portion.

If you change the data range for your chart quite often, it can get tiresome to continually pull up the Chart Wizard and change the data range reference. For instance, if you have a data table that includes several years worth of data, you may want to view a chart that is based on the first five years of data, and then change the data range so the chart refers to a different subset of the data. Make the changes often enough in the Chart Wizard, and you'll start casting about for ways to make the changes easier (and more reliably) than with the wizard.

One way to do this is with the use of named ranges and several worksheet functions. Let's say that your chart is embedded on a worksheet, but the worksheet is different than the one where the source data is located. On the same sheet as the chart, create two input cells which will serve as "from" and "to" indicators. Name these two cells something like FromYear and ToYear.

On your data worksheet (the one without the chart; I'll call it "Source Data"), the data is arranged with each year in a separate column and a series of cost factors in each row. Start your table in column F and place your years in row 2. Place the cost factors in column E, starting at row 3. Above the years place a capital letter that is the same as the column letter, and in column D place a number that is the same as the row number of the data.

D	E	F	G	H	I
		F	G	H	I
2		2006	2007	2008	2009
3	Cost1	69%	66.60%	73.90%	74.50%
4	Cost2	53.60%	56.90%	64.90%	64.40%
5	Cost3	59.30%	51.30%	62.70%	61.20%

First phase of data preparation

In this example, the chart that is embedded on the other worksheet is based on the data in the rangeF2:I5. There is nothing special about the chart, but the changes you are getting ready to make will make it dynamic, and therefore much more useful.

Start by placing the following formula in cell B1:

```
="Trends For " & IF(FromYear=ToYear,FromYear,FromYear & " to " & ToYear)
```

This formula provides a dynamic title that you will later use for your chart. Give cell B1 the name **addrTitle**, then place the following formula in cell B2:

```
="'Source Data'!$" & INDEX($F$1:$I$1,1,MATCH(FromYear,$F$2:$I$2)) & "$" & D2
& ":$" & INDEX($F$1:$I$1,1,MATCH(ToYear,$F$2:$I$2)) & "$" & D2
```

Copy the formula in B2 to the cells B3:B5. The formula returns address strings that represent the desired ranges for the X-axis values and the data series. The actual ranges returned by the formulas will vary, based on the values you enter in the FromYear and ToYear cells on the other worksheet. To make things clearer you can enter some labels into column A.

	A	B	C	D	E	F	G	H	I
1	Title	Trends For 2007 to 2009				F	G	H	I
2	Xvalues	'Source Data'!$G$2:$I$2		2		2006	2007	2008	2009
3	Cost1	'Source Data'!$G$3:$I$3		3	Cost1	69%	66.60%	73.90%	74.50%
4	Cost2	'Source Data'!$G$4:$I$4		4	Cost2	53.60%	56.90%	64.90%	64.40%
5	Cost3	'Source Data'!$G$5:$I$5		5	Cost3	59.30%	51.30%	62.70%	61.20%

Second phase of data preparation

Now you need to name each of the cells in the range B2:B5. Select B2 and in the Name Box (just above column A) enter the name "addrXVal" (without the quotes). Similarly name B3 as addrCost1, B4 as addrCost2, and B5 as addrCost3.

The next step is to create a couple of named formulas that you can use in creating the charts. Choose Insert | Name | Define to display the Define Name dialog box.

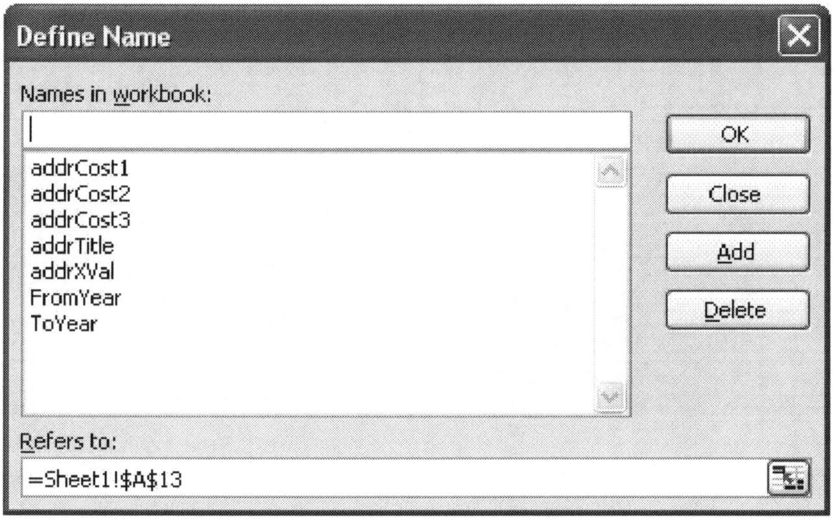

The Define Name dialog box.

In the name area, at the top of the dialog box, type "rngXVal" (without the quotes), then type the following in the Refers To box:

```
=INDIRECT(addrXVal)
```

Using the same dialog box, define additional names (rngCost1, rngCost2, and rngCost3) that use the same type of INDIRECT formula to refer to the ranges addrCost1, addrCost2, and addrCost3, respectively.

Now you are finally ready to update the references in your chart. Right-click the chart and select Source Data, then make sure the Series tab is displayed.

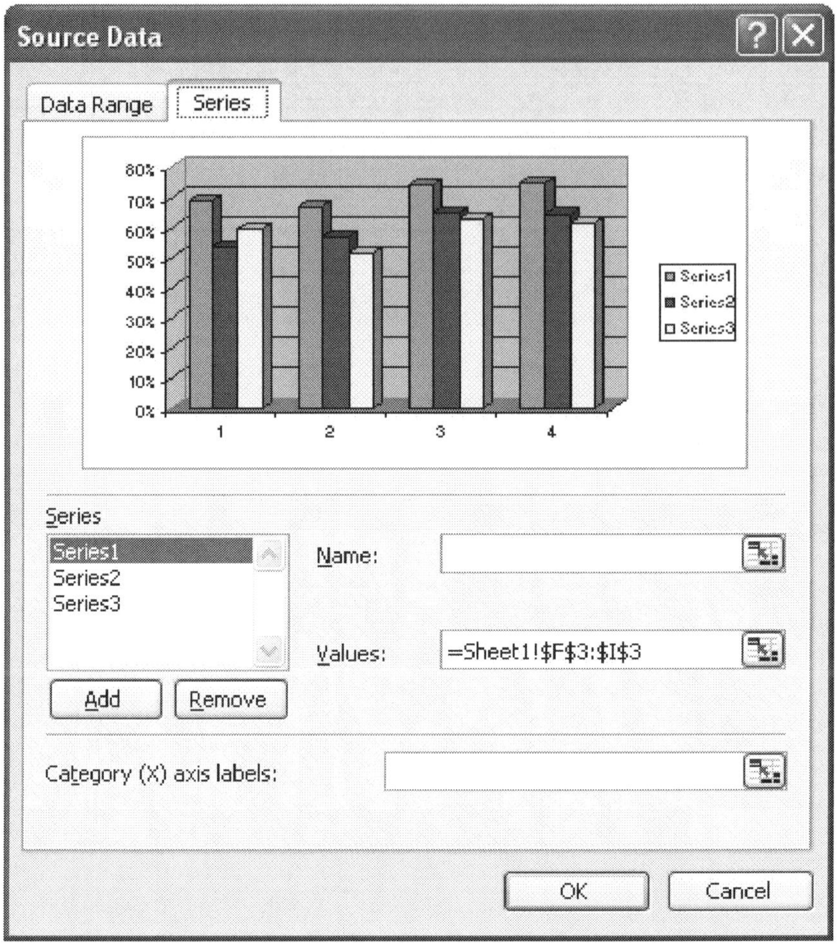

The Series tab of the Source Data dialog box.

For each of the data series listed at the left side of the dialog box, enter the Name and Values according to the names you defined. Thus, for the Cost1 series you would enter a Name of ='Source Data'!addrCost1 and a Values of ='Source Data'!rngCost1. You would use the similar references and names for each of the other data series, as well.

Note that you must include the name of your worksheet (Source Data), within apostrophes, in the references you enter. In the Category (X) Axis Labels reference you can enter ='Source Data'!rngXVal.

Once this is done, you can change the starting and ending years in the FromYear and ToYear cells, and Excel automatically and immediately updates the chart to represent the data you specified.

For an extra touch, if you haven't already added a chart title, go ahead and do so. Right-click the chart and select Chart Options, then display the Titles tab.

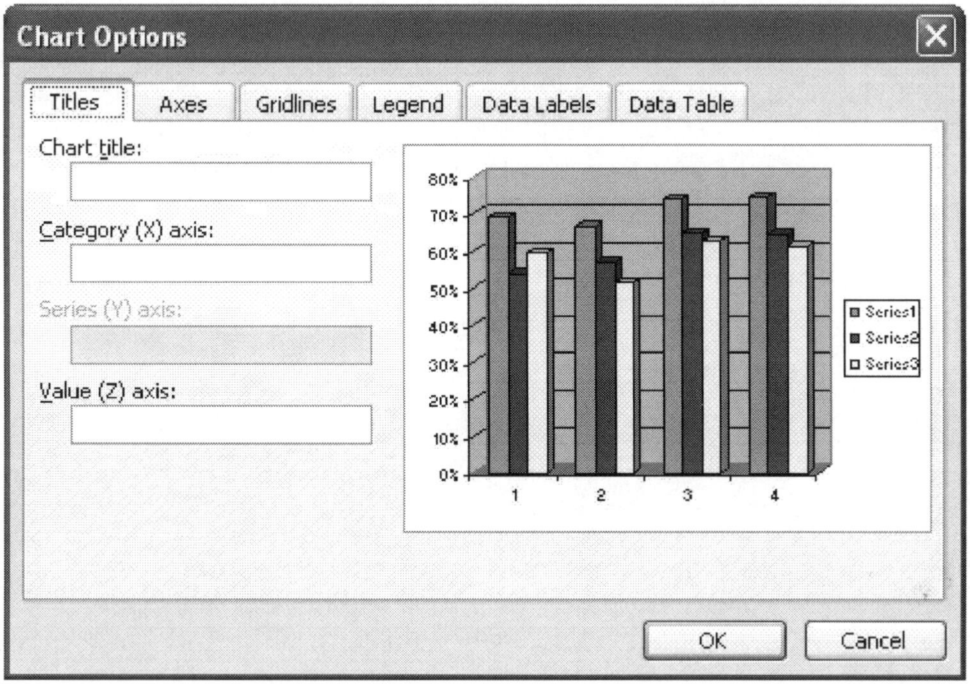

The Titles tab of the Chart Options dialog box.

Enter anything you'd like in the Chart Title box (you'll replace it in a moment), then click OK. The chart title should already be selected, but if it isn't, click on it once. You should see the selection box around the title. In the Formula bar enter the following:

```
='Source Data'!addrTitle
```

The chart title is now linked back to the cell containing the title string, which in turn is dynamically updated each time you change the FromYear and ToYear values.

Automatically Updating Charts for Additional Data

Excel shines at turning your data into charts—graphical representations of your data. You can easily create a chart based on a range of data in a worksheet. Normally, if you add additional data to your range, you will need to once again create the chart or at best change the range of cells on which the chart is based.

If you get tired of modifying charts to refer to new data ranges, there are a couple of shortcuts you can try out. The first shortcut works fine if you simply need to "fine tune" the range used in a chart. (This approach only works if the chart is on object on the same worksheet that contains the data on which the chart is based.) Follow these steps:

1. Enter any new data to the table on which the chart is based.
2. Select all the cells that you just entered.
3. Click anywhere on the selection border around the cells. (Don't click on the fill handle.)
4. Drag the selection toward the chart and drop it on the chart.

That's it—Excel incorporates the new data right into the existing chart, slick as a whistle.

Another approach is to add new data to the range not at the end, but somewhere within the range. For instance, you may have some data that represents a time period, such as 11/1 through 11/13, and you create a chart based on those dates. If you add new data to the end of the range (after 11/13), then Excel doesn't know you want those items added to the chart.

Instead, insert some blank rows somewhere within the data range; it doesn't matter where, as long as the record for 11/13 is below the added rows. You can then add the new data in the new rows, and the chart is automatically updated to include the data.

One drawback to this approach, of course, is that the inserted data will be out of order when compared to the overall structure of the data table. It is interesting to note that for some types of data—such as those based on dates—

Excel will automatically sort the data by date as it presents it in the chart, but not in the data table itself. You can always use Excel's sort feature to reorder the data in the table, all without affecting what is presented in the chart.

Still another approach is to create a "dynamic range." This approach works well if the data range you are charting is the only data on the worksheet. Follow these steps:

1. Create your data table as you normally would. (To keep things simple, we'll assume that you are creating a two-column data table, in columns A and B, that you then want to chart.)
2. Create your chart, as desired.
3. With the worksheet visible, choose Insert | Name | Define. Excel displays the Define Name dialog box.

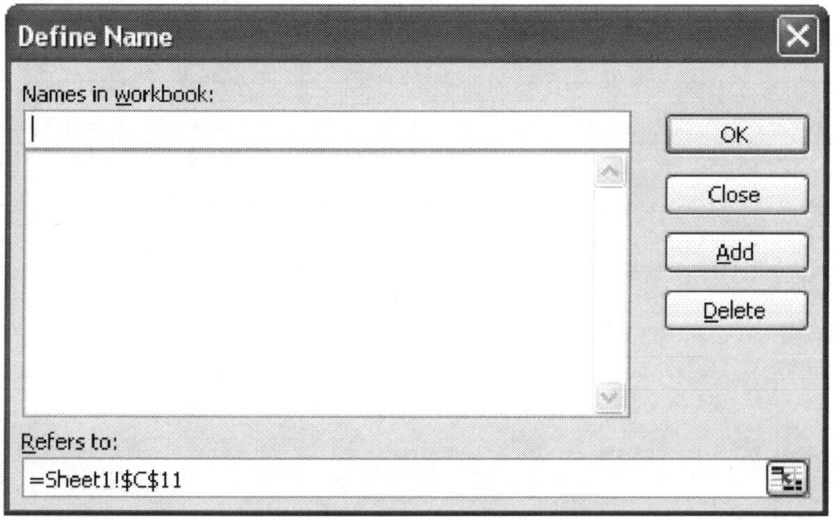

The Define Name dialog box.

4. In the Names in Workbook or Name field (depending on your version of Excel) enter a name that will refer to the data in column A.
5. In the Refers To field, enter the following formula. You should change the sheet name and beginning cell (in this case $A$2), as necessary. If you change the beginning cell, you should also change the final part of the formula (-1) to be one less than the row number of the

beginning cell. Thus, if you change the beginning cell to $A$5, you should change the final part of the formula to -4.

```
=OFFSET(Sheet1!$A$2,0,0,COUNTA(Sheet1! $A:$A)-1)
```

6. Click Add. Excel creates the name and associates it with the formula you entered. The Define Name dialog box should still be visible, with the newly defined name listed.
7. In the Names in Workbook or Name field (depending on your version of Excel) enter a name that will refer to the data in column B.
8. In the Refers To field, enter the following formula. (You should make the same type of changes to the sheet name, beginning cell, and final part of the formula as described in step 5.)

```
=OFFSET(Sheet1!$B$2,0,0,COUNTA(Sheet1!$B:$B)-1)
```

9. Click Add. Excel creates the name.
10. Click OK to close the Define Name dialog box.
11. Display the chart and select the data series. (There should only be one data series, since this is a simple two-column data table.) The formula bar will display a formula similar to the following:

```
=SERIES(Sheet1!$B$1,Sheet1!$A$2:$A$32, Sheet1!$B$2:$B$32,1)
```

12. Replace the ranges in the formula with the names you defined earlier in these steps. Assuming you defined the names ***Dates*** and ***Readings*** in steps 6 and 9, the formula should look like this:

```
=SERIES(,Sheet1!Dates,Sheet1!Readings,1)
```

Now the chart will update automatically regardless of where you add information in your data table. This works because the names you defined in steps 6 and 10 refer to a formula that calculates the extent of data in columns A and B of your worksheet.

There are many other ways that you can create dynamic ranges, depending on the characteristics of the data you are using. For additional information, see these Web resources:

```
http://j-walk.com/ss/excel/usertips/tip053.htm
http://www.ozgrid.com/Excel/DynamicRanges.htm
```

Multiple Data Points in a Chart Column

Jeff creates a lot of charts to track expenditures and labor by project. He creates stacked charts that show totals, but is looking for a way to combine stacked column and clustered column charts to provide just what he needs.

The solution is found in the way you organize the data in your worksheet. In short, you should leave a blank column (or row) between major groupings of your data. When you then create the chart, the blank area translates into a blank area on the chart, which makes it appear as if you have different clusters of data.

For a complete discussion of how this can be done, refer to the links at Jon Peltier's Web site. Jon is an Excel MVP, and has a good resource that speaks to this very issue:

```
http://www.peltiertech.com/Excel/ChartsHowTo/ClusterStack.html
```

Identifying Scatter Plot Points

Phil asked if it was possible to control exactly what information is shown as data labels in a scatter plot (xy) graph. It seems such functionality is not built directly into Excel. The best solutions involve the use of third-party add-ins to produce the desired results.

One highly recommended add-in is the XY Chart Labeler, created by Rob Bovey. You can find this free add-in here:

```
http://www.appspro.com/Utilities/ChartLabeler.htm
```

You can also find xy chart labeling features in some commercial add-ins, such as the Power Utility Pak by John Walkenbach:

```
http://spreadsheetpage.com/index.php/products/
```

Reading Values from Graphs

When creating charts from Excel data, you can smooth out the lines between data points by using any number of methods. At some point, you may want to actually figure out how Excel does its calculations to determine where to actually plot points along the line. Rather than visually trying to figure out where a point falls, you can follow these steps:

1. Right-click on the data series in question. Excel displays a Context menu.
2. Choose the Add Trendline option from the Context menu. Excel displays the Add Trendline dialog box.

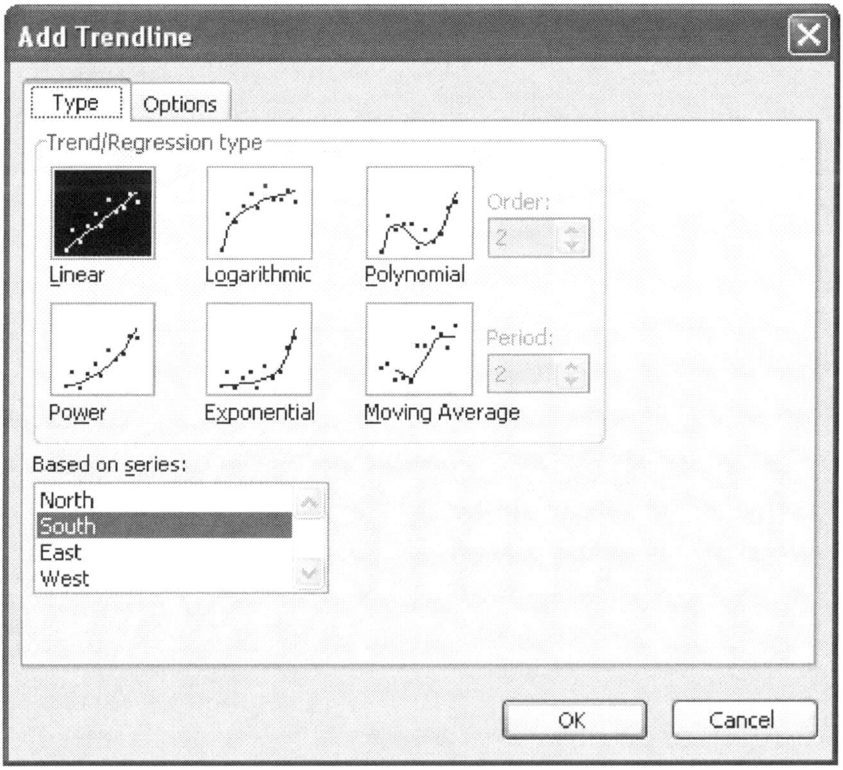

The Add Trendline dialog box.

3. Make sure the regression type you want to use is selected.
4. Display the Options tab.

5. Make sure the Display Equation on Chart check box is selected.
6. Click on OK.

The result is that Excel shows a formula, on the chart, that represents how it calculated each point along the line. You can then use this formula to determine points, as well. No more guessing! Once you know the formula, you can turn off the formula display if you want it off.

If you would like to know the different formulas that Excel uses for different types of trend lines, you can use the online Help system to search for "equations for calculating trendlines."

Noting a False Zero On a Chart

Stephe created a chart and, by using 'Format Axis/Scale,' limited the y-axis to show only the range from 400 to 450. This accentuates variation that would be almost invisible if his chart included the entire range from zero. He notes that this technique has a potential for misleading by exaggeration (whether deliberate or not). Therefore, there is a convention that a zig-zag should be inserted at the bottom of the y-axis to highlight the fact that a 'false zero' is being employed. Stephe wonders if there is a way to add this notation to an Excel chart.

There is not a way to add this indicator automatically. That means you could add one manually, by creating a small graphic with the symbol and then inserting the graphic at the appropriate place on the chart.

There are other approaches that could be used; some of the ideas from these websites may help:

```
http://peltiertech.com/Excel/Charts/BrokenYAxis.html
http://tushar-mehta.com/excel/newsgroups/broken_y_axis/tutorial/
```

Another approach might be to combine two charts based on different ranges of your data set. Follow these general steps:

1. Create your main chart based on all your data, without the adjustment to the y-axis.

2. Create a second, smaller chart showing only your desired range (400 to 450).
3. Position the second chart over the first chart (overlay it) so that it fits into an empty area of the first chart and doesn't hide any data points.
4. Format both charts as desired.
5. Group the two charts together so they are treated as a unit.

The benefit to this approach is that all your data is visible, a perception of skewing is eliminated, and people can still see the detail that you desire.

Negatives in Pie Charts

Excel allows you to easily create charts based on the data in a worksheet. If you create a pie chart, Excel charts negative values as if they were positive (in other words, it uses the absolute value). You may, however, prefer to have the negative values charted as if they were zero—to not have a slice of the pie.

Normally, people create pie charts based on a simple set of values. Each value within the series represents a portion of the whole. Thus, pie charts are often created based on the result of some sort of formula, such as the sum of values in a column; the sums of each column are the basis for the pie chart. Instead of using a standard SUM formula for the values to be charted, you could use a formula such as the following:

```
=IF(SUM(D7:D11)<0,0,SUM(D7:D11))
```

In this case, the value to be charted is set to zero if the sum is less than zero, or it reflects the actual total if the sum is zero or above.

If your data is conducive to filtering, you could also set up a filter so that negative values are filtered out. This will cause those values to be ignored in the chart created by Excel.

Of course, all this being said, one would have to wonder if a pie chart is the appropriate chart for representing this type of data in the first place. After all, pie charts represent portions of a whole—yet by filtering or adjusting totals, portions of the whole are being removed. Granted, they are negative portions, but they are portions nonetheless.

Pie charts, by their nature, are not well-suited for displaying negative numbers. If negative numbers are expected, then column or bar charts are a much more appropriate choice. Why? Because they can represent data that falls to the left of or below a baseline—as is appropriate for negative numbers.

Positive and Negative Colors in a Chart

Merril asked if there was a way to create a line chart so that when a line represented a negative value, the color of the line would change at the point when it went negative. For instance, in a particular data series, as long as the line represented positive values, it would be blue, but when the line represented negative values, it would change to red.

Unfortunately there is no way to easily do this in Excel. There are, however, a couple of workarounds you can try. The first is to use a macro to change the line colors of chart lines that represent negative values. The following macro is an example of such an approach:

```
Sub PosNegLine()
    Dim chtSeries As Series
    Dim SeriesNum As Integer
    Dim SeriesColor As Integer
    Dim MyChart As Chart
    Dim R As Range
    Dim i As Integer
    Dim LineColor As Integer
    Dim PosColor As Integer
    Dim NegColor As Integer
    Dim LastPtColor As Integer
    Dim CurrPtColor As Integer

    PosColor = 4 'Green
    NegColor = 3 'red
    SeriesNum = 1

    Set MyChart = ActiveSheet.ChartObjects(1).Chart
    Set chtSeries = MyChart.SeriesCollection(SeriesNum)
    Set R = GetChartRange(MyChart, 1, "Values")
```

```
    For i = 2 To R.Cells.Count
        LastPtColor = IIf(R.Cells(i - 1).Value < 0, NegColor, PosColor)
        CurrPtColor = IIf(R.Cells(i).Value < 0, NegColor, PosColor)

        If LastPtColor = CurrPtColor Then
            LineColor = LastPtColor
        Else
            If Abs(R.Cells(i - 1).Value) > Abs(R.Cells(i).Value) Then
                LineColor = LastPtColor
            Else
                LineColor = CurrPtColor
            End If
        End If
        chtSeries.Points(i).Border.ColorIndex = LineColor
    Next i
End Sub

Function GetChartRange(Ch As Chart, Ser As Integer, _
  ValXorY As String) As Range
    Dim SeriesFormula As String
    Dim ListSep As String * 1
    Dim Pos As Integer
    Dim LSeps() As Integer
    Dim Txt As String
    Dim i As Integer

    Set GetChartRange = Nothing

    On Error Resume Next
        SeriesFormula = Ch.SeriesCollection(Ser).Formula
    ListSep = ","
    For i = 1 To Len(SeriesFormula)
        If Mid$(SeriesFormula, i, 1) = ListSep Then
            Pos = Pos + 1
            ReDim Preserve LSeps(Pos)
            LSeps(Pos) = i
        End If
    Next i

    If UCase(ValXorY) = "XVALUES" Then
        Txt = Mid$(SeriesFormula, LSeps(1) + 1, LSeps(2) - LSeps(1) - 1)

        Set GetChartRange = Range(Txt)
    End If

    If UCase(ValXorY) = "VALUES" Then
        Txt = Mid$(SeriesFormula, LSeps(2) + 1, LSeps(3) - LSeps(2) - 1)

        Set GetChartRange = Range(Txt)
    End If
End Function
```

When you select a chart and then run the PosNegLine macro, it looks through the chart and, for line segments between negative data point values, changes the line color to red. For line segments connecting positive data points, the line color is set to green.

The problem with this solution is that it provides only an approximation; it only works with lines connecting two data points, and it can either change the entire line segment or not. If the beginning data point is positive and the ending data point is negative, it cannot change the color of a line right as it passes into negative values.

Another approach is to format data points as different colors or shapes, based on whether they are positive or negative. A way to accomplish this is detailed at Jon Peltier's Web site, located here:

```
http://www.peltiertech.com/Excel/Charts/ConditionalChart1.html
```

Converting Charts to GIF Files

Conrad has an Excel chart that he would like to share with others. He's determined that the best way for him to do this is to share it as a GIF image file. He isn't sure how to create a GIF file from an Excel chart, however.

There are a couple of things you can do to get the file you want. If you only need to create a GIF file once in a while, the best be would be to simply use a graphics program. For instance, you could follow these simple steps:

1. Start a graphics program such as Paint.
2. Switch back to Excel and display your chart as you normally would.
3. Right-click the chart and choose Copy from the resulting Context menu. This copies the chart to the Clipboard.
4. Switch to the graphics program.
5. Press **Ctrl+V** to paste the chart into the graphics program.
6. Make any changes to the image that you want.
7. Save the image as a GIF file.

If you prefer, you could modify these steps a bit (well, steps 2 and 3) to capture an entire screen instead of just the chart. This allows you to size the chart any way you want prior to capture, even filling the entire screen, if desired. To capture the screen, just press the **PrtScrn** button on your keyboard, which places the screen capture in the Clipboard. You can then use steps 4 through 7 to put the screen into Paint and crop it or make other edits you need.

If you need to save your charts as GIF files quite often, then the best solution is to use a macro. The following simple macro saves the currently selected chart as a GIF file in the same directory in which the current workbook is stored.

```
Sub SaveChartAsGIF()
    Dim sFileName As String
    sFileName = ThisWorkbook.Path & "\" & ActiveChart.Name & ".gif"
    ActiveChart.Export Filename:=sFileName, FilterName:="GIF"
End Sub
```

The use of the Export method to save out charts is detailed in this Microsoft Knowledgebase article:

```
http://support.microsoft.com/?kbid=163103
```

The article indicates that it is written for Excel 97, but the coding will work just fine with all versions of Excel that use VBA.

If you want a more full-featured macro approach, this article on Jon Peltier's site is quite helpful:

```
http://peltiertech.com/WordPress/enhanced-export-chart-procedure/
```

Excel Charts in PowerPoint

If you do a lot of presentations, you may deal with many large data reports that include charts and graphs that summarize data for your audiences. Sometimes you may need to add these charts and graphs to PowerPoint presentations.

The problem with doing a simple copy and paste of a chart from Excel to PowerPoint is that although you only see the chart in the PowerPoint slide, the entire workbook is copied into PowerPoint as well. If someone double-clicks the chart in the slide, PowerPoint will open the entire Excel workbook.

This poses a couple of problems. First, unless the PowerPoint file has been password protected (not really an option for mass distribution) a user could easily adjust the data feeding into the chart and corrupt accuracy.

Secondly, since the entire Excel workbook is copied into the PowerPoint file, this can dramatically increase the total size on the PowerPoint file, possibly making it too cumbersome for distribution.

One simple solution is to modify how the pasting into PowerPoint is done. Follow these steps:

1. In Excel, copy the chart as you normally would. (For instance, select the chart and press **Ctrl+C**.)
2. In PowerPoint, display the slide where you want the chart to appear.
3. Choose Paste Special from the Edit menu. PowerPoint displays the Paste Special dialog box.

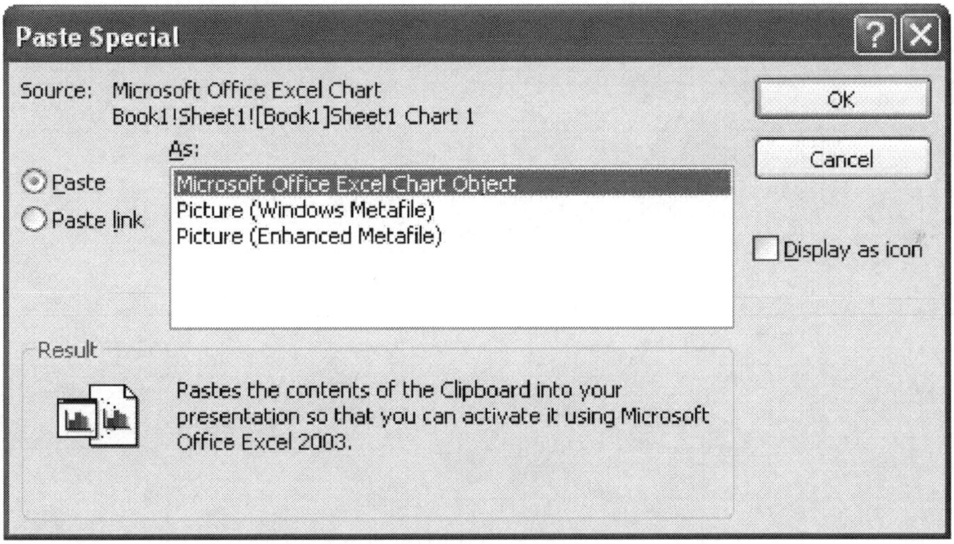

The Paste Special dialog box in PowerPoint.

4. Select the Picture option.
5. Click OK.

This time, only the image of the chart is pasted into the slide. This maintains the accuracy and security of your chart and significantly reduces the size of your PowerPoint presentation.

Embedding an Excel Chart in a Word Document

Most of the time, Microsoft Office applications work fairly well together. For instance, you might be creating a report for a presentation, and you need to include a chart along with the report. Fortunately, you can embed an Excel chart directly within a report you happen to be creating in Word. This is done in the following manner:

1. Select the Excel chart you wish to embed in your Word document. (Make sure you select the entire chart, and not just a portion of it.)
2. Press **CTRL+C** to copy the chart to the Clipboard.
3. Switch to the Word document.
4. Position the insertion pointer where you want the chart placed.
5. Choose Paste Special from the Edit menu. The Paste Special dialog box appears.

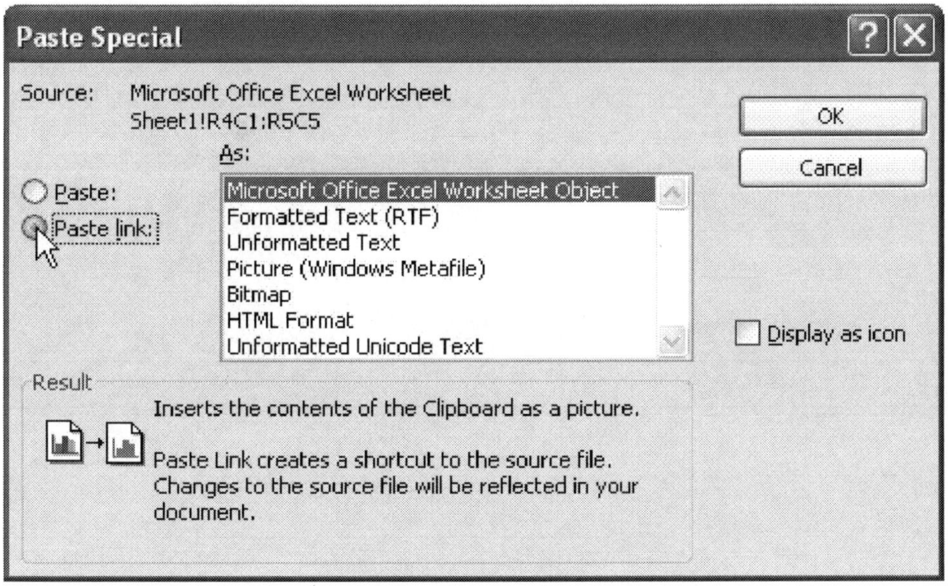

The Paste Special dialog box.

6. Select the Microsoft Excel Chart Object or Microsoft Office Excel Chart Object (depending on your version of Word) as the preferred method of pasting.
7. Make sure the Paste Link radio button is selected.
8. Click on OK. Word inserts the linked chart in your document.

14

Printing Charts

Printing a Chart

Excel allows you to quickly convert your worksheet data into snazzy charts. (You know—a picture is worth a thousand worksheet cells.) Once your chart looks just the way you want it to, you may be wondering exactly how to get the best results when printing it. In many ways, printing a chart is the same as printing a worksheet, but with a few subtle differences.

If you are not printing to a color printer, the first thing you will want to do is make sure you use the Print Preview feature to see what your chart will appear like in black and white. If there is not enough contrast between different parts of your chart, you will want to make changes to either the colors or patterns used within the chart so there is a better contrast and your printed chart will look better.

When you are ready to print your chart, the easiest method is to simply press **Ctrl+P**. Excel displays the Print dialog box, with which you are probably already familiar. The information at the top of the dialog box indicates where your chart will be printed. If this is not the printer you want to use, choose a different printer using the drop-down list.

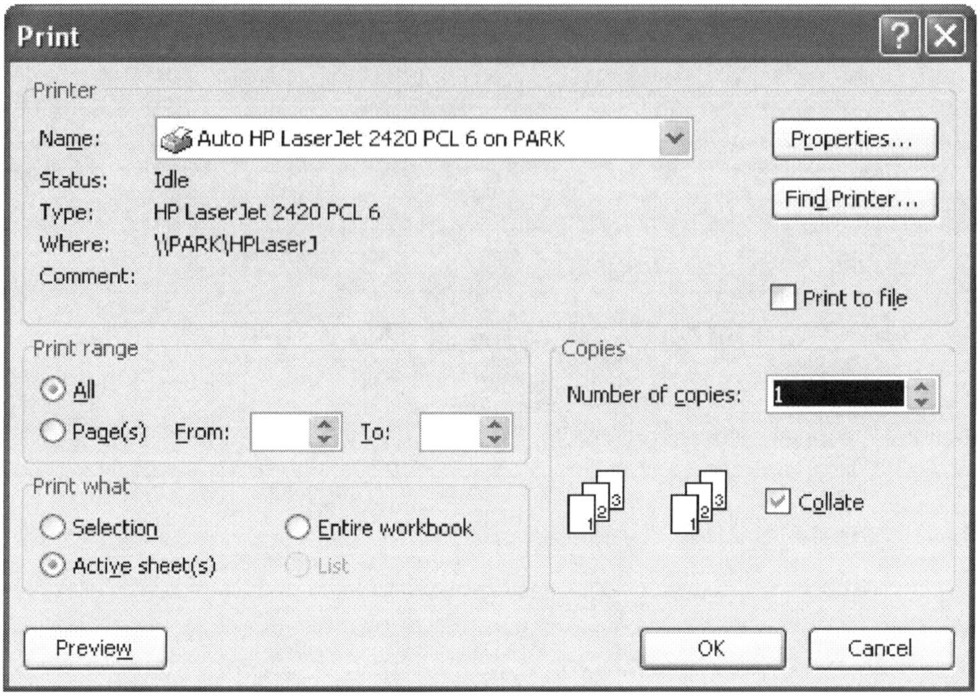

The Print dialog box.

The actual information and options available in the Print dialog box can vary depending on the type of printer you are using. Different printers have different capabilities, and Windows takes advantage of these capabilities as much as possible. In general, however, you can use this dialog box to select the number of copies you want to print, along with which pages you want to print.

One of the other things you can specify is what you want sent to the printer. This is done by making a selection in the Print What box. By default, this field is set to Active Sheet(s), typically meaning that only the current worksheet will be printed (the one containing your chart). By changing this field, you can also specify that only a Selection be printed or that your Entire Workbook is printed. (You should note that the Selection option will only be available if you are printing a worksheet containing an embedded chart; it is not available when printing a chart sheet.)

When you are satisfied with what you want to print, click on the OK button. Excel sends your information to the printer, as you have directed.

Preparing a Chart Sheet for Printing

Excel allows you to use two types of charts: embedded charts and chart sheets. Since an embedded chart is included as part of a regular worksheet, you can print one just as you would any other worksheet.

Chart sheets, on the other hand, take a bit more preparation in order to print. To modify how a chart sheet appears, display the Page Setup dialog box (File | Page Setup). Make sure you select the Chart tab; there you can select the quality of the printout and specify how much of the printed page the chart should occupy. (The options available in the dialog box depend on the version of Excel you are using.)

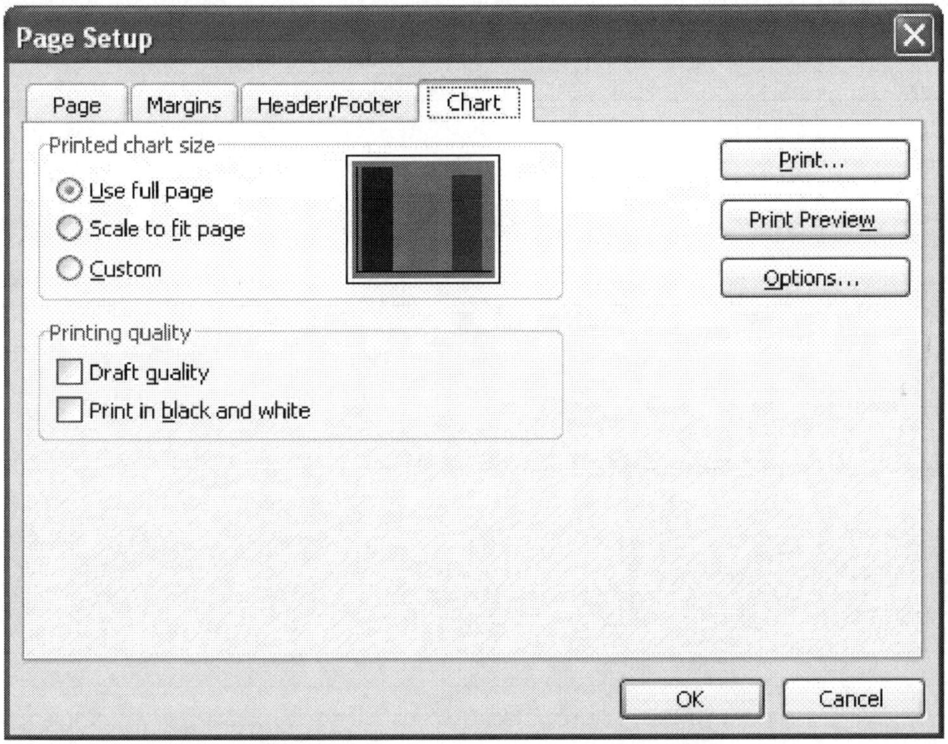

The Chart tab of the Page Setup dialog box.

You can specify the size of the printed chart. Since a chart sheet is, by nature, an entire sheet of paper, the default selection is Use Full Page. You can also choose either of the other options (Scale to Fit Page or Custom) to specify a different page size, however. If you choose either of these options and click on OK, Excel places a dashed line around the chart area. If you use the mouse to click on this line, sizing handles will appear around the image.

As with any other graphics image, you can size the chart sheet. As you move the mouse pointer over the sizing handles, it changes to a sizing arrow. Click on a sizing handle and drag the border of the chart to reflect the size you want to use. The direction of the arrowheads indicates the direction you can move the border. When you release the mouse button, the chart is resized and redrawn automatically.

Printing a Chart Across Multiple Pages

If you are using Excel to chart very large amounts of data, the charts you create can end up being very large, as well. This leads to a problem when printing the chart: Do you print it so it fits on one piece of paper, thereby losing detail, or do you try to maintain the detail and print the chart on multiple pieces of paper?

Unfortunately, the answer to what could otherwise be a simple question is complicated by the fact that Excel doesn't easily allow you to print a single chart across multiple pieces of papers. Instead you are left work around the problem. Fortunately, there are a few things you can do.

First of all, you could simply break the data range you are charting into smaller "chunks" of data that would be printed on different charts. Thus, the amount of detail on each chart would depend on the amount of data you are assigning to that chart. For instance, if the data range you want to actually chart is in A1:B2000, you might create 20 charts, with each chart made up of the data from 100 rows.

Another potential solution involves how you create the chart itself. Instead of creating the chart as a chart sheet, create it as an object on a worksheet. This results in a chart that floats over the top of the worksheet. You can then size the chart to be as wide as you want, thereby revealing as much data as you want. When you print the worksheet, Excel splits the chart across multiple pages, as desired.

There are two things to remember in this approach: First, you must make sure that you select a workbook cell when printing. If you select the chart before printing, Excel will print just the chart and shrink it to fit on a single page. Second, Excel will also try to print your large data range in the printout. To overcome this, you can play with the settings in the Print dialog box to get just the pages printed that you need.

Turning on Placeholders

If you are working with a large worksheet that has a large number of graphics, you may have noticed that Excel slows down quite a bit when displaying the graphics. This can be particularly distracting, especially if your graphics are quite detailed or are being loaded across a busy network connection.

You can speed up the display of your worksheet by using placeholders. This results in Excel displaying boxes where your graphics would normally appear. This means that Excel does not have to redisplay the complete graphic, and therefore your display will be much faster. To turn on placeholders, follow these steps:

1. Choose Options from the Tools menu. You will see the Options dialog box.
2. Click on the View tab.

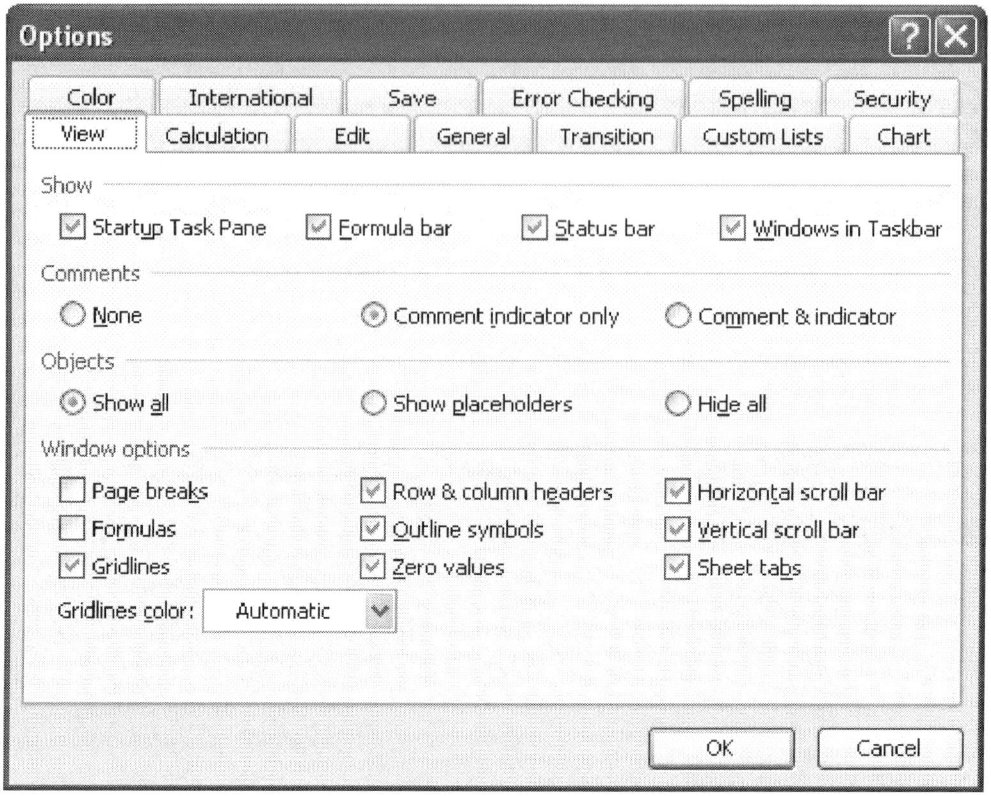

The View tab of the Options dialog box.

3. Use the Show Placeholders check box to control whether placeholders are used by Excel. Click on the check box to turn the capability on and off; a check in the box means placeholders are enabled.
4. Click on OK.

Exporting Black and White Charts

Excel allows you to create charts in full color. When you get ready to print the chart, you can instruct Excel to print it in "black and white" (via File | Page Setup | Chart | Print in Black and White). You may wonder if there is a way to export this "black and white" version of the chart, so that you can work with it in a different program.

The answer is that you cannot do this, at least not directly. To understand why this is, you must understand how the "print in black and white" feature works. This feature only affects what is sent to the printer driver (to your printer), it doesn't affect the actual chart at all. Even when you click on Print Preview, you are not viewing your actual chart, but a representation of what your chart will look like when printed. Thus, you are seeing printer output, not the real chart.

If you want to export a black and white version of your chart, there are several ways to accomplish the task. The first is to simply view the chart in Print Preview and do a screen capture (press **ALT+PRINT SCREEN**). You can then paste the screen into your favorite graphics program and touch it up, as desired.

If you want to export the chart instead of just capturing the screen, then you should change the colors of the chart so that they really are grayscale and contain the same patterns you would see if you chose to print in black and white. This approach actually changes the source for the chart, rather than relying on Excel to do a transformation of the chart when you print. Once you get done making the formatting changes you can even save the chart as a "chart type" so you can use it as a pattern for other charts you create.

If desired, you can also use a macro to convert between color and grayscale chart presentation. This approach is highly dependent on the colors you want to use in the chart, the type of chart you are using, and the number of data series in the chart. The following is an example of a macro that will toggle the colors in a data series between color and black and white, for up to five data series.

```
Option Explicit
Public bColored As Integer

Sub ColoredToBW()
    Dim cht As Chart
    Dim chtSC As SeriesCollection
    Dim x As Integer
    Dim iSeriesCount As Integer
    Dim iColors(1 To 5, 0 To 1) As Integer
    Dim iColor As Integer

'Set colors for BW series
    iColors(1, 0) = 1 'Black
    iColors(2, 0) = 56 'Gray-80%
    iColors(3, 0) = 16 'Gray-50%
```

```
        iColors(4, 0) = 48 'Gray-40%
        iColors(5, 0) = 15 'Gray-25%

    'Set colors for Color series
        iColors(1, 1) = 55 'Indigo
        iColors(2, 1) = 7 'pink
        iColors(3, 1) = 6 'yellow
        iColors(4, 1) = 8 'Turquoise
        iColors(5, 1) = 13 'Violet

    'Toggle Color/BW change 0 to 1 or 1 to 0
        bColored = 1 - bColored

        Set cht = ActiveChart

    'check that a chart is selected
        If cht Is Nothing Then
            MsgBox ("Select a chart")
            Exit Sub
        End If

        Set chtSC = cht.SeriesCollection

        'Check for MIN of number of series or
        'colors and only do the minimum
        iSeriesCount = Application.WorksheetFunction.Min _
          (UBound(iColors), chtSC.Count)

        For x = 1 To iSeriesCount
            'Define the color
            iColor = iColors(x, bColored)

            'Set the LINE color
            chtSC(x).Border.ColorIndex = iColor

            'Marker color
            With chtSC(x)
                .MarkerBackgroundColorIndex = xlNone
                .MarkerForegroundColorIndex = iColor
            End With
        Next x
    End Sub
```

This example will not work with all chart types; you will need to modify it to reflect your needs. It will, however, serve as a starting point for making your own macro.

15

Using Macros with Charts

Creating Charts in VBA

Excel is very handy at creating charts from data in a worksheet. What if you want to create a chart directly from VBA, without using any data in a worksheet? You can do this by "fooling" Excel into thinking it is working with information from a worksheet, and then providing your own. The following macro illustrates this concept:

```
Sub MakeChart()
    'Add a new chart
    Charts.Add

    'Set the dummy data range for the chart
    ActiveChart.SetSourceData Sheets("Sheet1").Range("a1:d4"), _
      PlotBy:=xlColumns

    'Manually set the values for the data series
    ActiveChart.SeriesCollection(1).Formula = _
      "=SERIES(""First Data"",{""a"",""b"",""c"",""d""},{2,3,4,5},1)"
    ActiveChart.SeriesCollection(2).Formula = _
      "=SERIES(""Second Data"",{""a"",""b"",""c"",""d""},{6,7,8,9},2)"
    ActiveChart.SeriesCollection(3).Formula = _
      "=SERIES(""Third Data"",{""a"",""b"",""c"",""d""},{10,11,12,13},3)"
End Sub
```

The comments in this example explain what is going on for each step. When setting the dummy data range, the SetSourceData method assumes the range is on a worksheet named Sheet1. If you don't have such a sheet in your workbook, you need to alter the command accordingly.

Later, when manually setting the values for the data series, the SERIES command is used to specify the label for the series (First Data, Second Data, and Third Data), the array of category labels (a, b, c, and d in all series), the array of values for the series, and a number specifying which series number this represents.

Specifying Chart Sizes

Megan has a monthly report that she creates in Excel. She has most of the report automated, except for one annoying problem that she must handle manually. The report includes four pie charts used to illustrate some values from the report. Each pie chart comes out a bit different in size, and the manual task is that Megan needs to make them all the same size. She wants each of them to be 5 centimeters square, and would love a way to remove the manual drudgery of formatting them each month.

The reason that each of the pie charts is a little bit different in size is because when you create a chart with the default settings, Excel decides it can adjust the chart size as it sees fit. This sizing can depend on several factors, such as available space, label sizes, number of data points, etc. One way to improve the chances that each chart will be the same size is to create your first chart and then use **Ctrl+C** and **Ctrl+V** to copy the chart the other three times. Each should be identical, and then you can adjust the data ranges reflected in the charts so that they display the desired ranges.

If it is not practical to copy and paste the charts (for instance, if the charts are created by macros), then you may be interested in just using a quick macro to adjust the size of all the charts in the worksheet. The following macro will step through each chart and adjust the Height and Width properties to 5 centimeters.

```
Sub AdjChartSizes()
    Dim cht As ChartObject
    For Each cht In ActiveSheet.ChartObjects
        cht.Chart.ChartArea.AutoScaleFont = False
        cht.Height = Application.CentimetersToPoints(5)
        cht.Width = Application.CentimetersToPoints(5)
    Next cht
End Sub
```

Specifying the Size of Chart Objects

When you create an Excel chart, as an object to be placed in a worksheet, the chart object is automatically sized to fit one-quarter of the screen size. You may not want the chart object to be this particular size. For instance, you may want your chart objects to always be a standard size, so they always appear the same relative to your worksheets.

There is no way to specify a chart object size as you are creating the chart. You can, however, resize the chart object after it is created, just as you can resize other graphic elements of your worksheet. You could write a macro to create the object at a particular size, but doing so would remove much of the flexibility that is inherent in the Chart wizard. For instance, when you specify the size of the chart object being created, you also have to specify other characteristics, such as chart type. It is easier to pick and choose such characteristics through the Chart wizard than it is to do so in a macro.

You can, however, easily create a macro that will resize an existing chart object. The key commands of such a macro would be changing the Width and Height properties for the chart object. In VBA, these properties are specified in points. Thus, if you wanted to resize the chart object so it was 4 inches high, you would set the Height property to 288, which is the number of points in 4 inches (4 * 72).

The following macro gives an example of one way to step through all the chart objects on a worksheet and make them the same size.

```
Sub ResizeCharts()
    For j = 1 To ActiveSheet.Shapes.Count
        If ActiveSheet.Shapes(j).Type = msoChart Then
            ActiveSheet.Shapes(j).Width = 4 * 72
            ActiveSheet.Shapes(j).Height = 3 * 72
        End If
    Next j
End Sub
```

This particular macro sets the width of each chart object to 4 inches, and the height to 3 inches. If you are looking for a free third-party solution to resizing charts—along with performing other common tasks on charts—then consider Chart Tools, written by John Walkenbach. You can find it here:

```
http://j-walk.com/ss/excel/files/charttools.htm
```

Unlocking Charts

A common task done in macros is to lock and unlock different cells and objects in a workbook. This is often done for protection reasons, so that things cannot be modified inadvertently by users. If you need to unlock the charts that are in your workbook, you can easily do so if you remember that even though charts can be considered drawing objects, you don't unlock them as drawing objects—you specifically unlock the chart object.

In addition, how you unlock a chart depends on whether it is a Chart sheet or a Chart object on a regular worksheet. The following code, named ChartUnProtect, provides an example of how to successfully unprotect both types of charts.

```
Sub ChartUnProtect()
    Dim wks As Worksheet
    Dim cht As Chart
    Dim chtObj As ChartObject
    Dim PW As String
    PW = "mypass"

    'Unprotect all Chart sheets
    For Each cht In ActiveWorkbook.Charts
        Sheets(cht.Name).Unprotect password:=PW
    Next

    'Unlock all Chart objects on each worksheet
    For Each wks In ActiveWorkbook.Worksheets
        wks.Unprotect password:=PW
        For Each chtObj In wks.ChartObjects
            wks.DrawingObjects(chtObj.Name).Locked = False
        Next
        wks.Protect password:=PW
    Next
End Sub
```

Changing Elements in Lots of Charts at One Time

Chris has a workbook that contains a lot of small, identical charts. He wants to change some of the attributes of elements in each chart—such as color or font size—all at one time.

If you find yourself using a "non-default" chart often (which means changing the appearance of certain chart elements after the chart is created), then a great approach is to create a custom chart and save that format in Excel. You can then use the saved format to create all your new charts, thereby minimizing the amount of later formatting you need to do. How you save custom chart formats has been covered in other issues of ***ExcelTips.***

Custom chart formats may be great for the future, but it doesn't help if you already have a whole bunch of charts in an existing workbook. In that case, the best solution is to use a macro which can step through all the charts in a workbook and make a desired change. You just need to decide up front which items you wish to change, and then program the macro to specifically change those items.

For example, the following macro changes the font color and size of the Y-axis labels. It loops through all the charts in the workbook, both sheets and embedded charts.

```
Sub ChangeAllCharts1()
    Dim cht As Chart
    Dim sht
    Dim ChtObj As ChartObject

    For Each cht In ActiveWorkbook.Charts
        With cht.Axes(xlValue).TickLabels.Font
            .Size = 20
            .Color = vbRed
        End With
    Next

    For Each sht In ActiveWorkbook.Sheets
        For Each ChtObj In sht.ChartObjects
            With ChtObj.Chart.Axes(xlValue).TickLabels.Font
                .Size = 20
                .Color = vbRed
            End With
```

```
        Next
    Next
End Sub
```

As written here, the macro changes the font size to 20 and the color to red. If you want the macro to change other elements, all you need to do is change the With statements to reflect the elements you want changed, or you could use a For...Next loop to step through all the chart elements. The following macro exhibits this technique, changing the background color of the charts in a workbook.

```
Sub ChangeAllCharts2()
    On Error Resume Next
    NewChartAreaColor = 34

    For J = 1 To ActiveWorkbook.Charts.Count
        ActiveWorkbook.Charts(J).Select

        'The pairs of line code indicate desired changes
        ActiveChart.ChartArea.Select
        Selection.Interior.ColorIndex = NewChartAreaColor
    Next J

    For J = 1 To ActiveWorkbook.Sheets.Count
        For K = 1 To Sheets(J).ChartObjects.Count
            Sheets(J).Select
            Sheets(J).ChartObjects(K).Activate

            'The pairs of line code indicate desired changes
            ActiveChart.ChartArea.Select
            Selection.Interior.ColorIndex = NewChartAreaColor
        Next K
    Next J
End Sub
```

Hyperlinks to Charts

Excel allows you to create hyperlinks, either to resources on the Internet or to cells in other worksheets. Excel won't, unfortunately, allow you to create hyperlinks that display chart sheets in your workbook. If a worksheet includes a chart object (the chart was created as an object in a worksheet), then you can create a hyperlink that displays the worksheet on which the chart object is located. You cannot, however, use an actual chart sheet as the target of your hyperlink.

The way to work around this problem is to create a macro that actually displays the desired chart sheet. You can then assign the macro to a button, a menu item, a toolbar button, or any similar object. You would use a macro such as the following:

```
Sub GotoChart1()
    Sheets("Chart1").Select
End Sub
```

This is a very simplistic version of a macro that displays a specific chart sheet. In this case, the chart sheet is named Chart1; you can change the name to reflect your needs. You can create a macro like this for each destination chart sheet in your workbook.

An alternative is to enhance the macro so that it accepts a parameter indicating the name of the chart sheet you want selected. For instance, consider the following macro:

```
Sub GotoChart2()
    Sheets(ActiveSheet.Shapes(Application.Caller) _
      .TopLeftCell.Value).Select
End Sub
```

With this macro in place, go back to your worksheet and select the cell where you want your hyperlink. Type the name of the chart sheet, and format it to look like a hyperlink. (Blue, underlined text, or formatted as desired. You are simulating a hyperlink; you are not creating a real one.)

Using the Forms toolbar, create a label object within the same cell, and format the label to not be visible. You do this by modifying the properties of the object so it has no lines, no text, etc. Then, right-click the label object and use the Assign Macro choice to assign the GotoChart2 macro to the object.

Now, when someone tries to click the "hyperlink," they are really clicking the invisible label object, and the macro is being executed. The macro determines the name of the object that called it (Application.caller), figures out what cell the object's top-left corner is in, and grabs the value of that cell. The value is then used as the destination name for the desired chart sheet.

Discover the Power in Excel!

Books, e-books, and CDs from Tips.Net

Amazing Array Formulas

An array is a group of items that can, in some fashion, be treated as a whole. In Excel, an array formula is a special type of formula that allows you to perform calculations on huge amounts of data, in a single operation. Array formulas, once properly understood, provide new and exciting ways that you can perform calculations with your data—some that would otherwise be impossible with regular Excel formulas.

In the pages of *ExcelTips: Amazing Array Formulas* you'll discover not only what array functions are and how to create them, but also dozens of different ways you can use them right away.

Excel 2003 Conditional Formatting

The conditional formatting capabilities of Excel are impressive and can be very powerful. All you need to do is picture how you want your data to appear, and then figure out the criteria that should be met in order for the formatting to be applied. Whenever the values change on which your conditional formatting is based, Excel changes the formatting to reflect those changed values.

Excel allows most of its formatting power to be applied based on the criteria you dream up. *Excel 2003 Conditional Formatting* presents everything you need to know to put conditional formatting to work with your data.

Excel 2003 Filters and Filtering

Filtering your data means displaying only a part of it. You provide the criteria that Excel should use to determine what gets displayed, and Excel helpfully displays just that data. Filtering is especially useful if you have a large data list and you want to work with only a subset of the records in that list.

Excel 2003 Filters and Filtering helps you manage your data effectively and efficiently. It provides the information you need to understand how both of Excel's filtering tools work and how you can use those tools with the real-world data you need to process. Get a grip on your data with *Excel 2003 Filters and Filtering!*

Excel 2003 Graphics and Charts

Many people, especially when they are new to Excel, create worksheets that contain only numbers, text, and formulas. Excel worksheets can contain much more than these elemental items. You can add all sorts of graphics to your worksheets or you can create amazing charts from your data. These items—graphics and charts—can liven up your data and provide some exciting ways to make your information mean even more.

Excel 2003 Graphics and Charts focuses on what you need to know to understand and put graphics and charts to work right away. You'll discover ways to stretch your knowledge and enhance how you can present the data in your worksheets.

Excel 2003 PivotTables for the Faint of Heart

For many people, the mere mention of "PivotTables" sends shivers up their spine. To some, the PivotTable is one of those tools in Excel that is best left some mythical (and mystical) expert, perhaps locked away in some ivory tower. For such folks, the PivotTable remains the most esoteric and exotic of Excel's analysis tools.

PivotTables don't need to be so scary, and they certainly don't need to be relegated to the realm of the esoteric or exotic. With *Excel 2003 PivotTables for the Faint of Heart* you can start using PivotTables right away to crunch the numbers you need to crunch and discover the answers hidden in your data.

Visit http://store.tips.net for more great Tips.Net titles!

Excel 2003 Serious Sorting

Using Excel you can manage data in a variety of ways with a number of tools. One commonly used Excel tool is embodied within its sorting capabilities. Excel allows you to easy and quickly sort data in just about any manner you can conceive.

Even though sorting data may be a routine task in Excel, many people still don't have a firm grasp on how to use the program's sorting capabilities fully. Even those who have been using the program for years and years often get into a rut and fail to recognize or take advantage of the full sorting power inherent in Excel.

Excel 2003 Serious Sorting discusses how you can use all the sorting capabilities provided in Excel, perhaps in ways you've never before considered.

ExcelTips: The Macros

Want to master Excel and make it adapt to what you want done? Then you need to discover the power of macros. Macros are a great way to expand the utility of Excel and the ways you can use the program.

ExcelTips: The Macros is designed for those wanting to learn how to create, use, and expand their understanding of Excel macros. In its pages you uncover how to make your use of Excel even more productive. It is the largest, most in-depth exploration of macros available anywhere!

Powerful Lookup Functions

Excel provides hundreds of worksheet functions you can use to build formulas, modify data, and get just the information you need in a cell. Of all the worksheet functions available, few are more powerful than Excel's lookup functions. They literally allow you to "look up" information based upon parameters you specify.

The pages of *ExcelTips: Powerful Lookup Functions* focus on dozens of tips that can help you better understand not only what lookup functions are, but how to use them in real-world scenarios to improve the calculations you must do in your own workbooks.

Times and Dates

Many people use Excel to enter, process, calculate, format, and display dates or times. *ExcelTips: Times and Dates* is designed to help you figure out just what to do with the times and dates stuck in your worksheets. No matter how you need to work with dates and times, *ExcelTips: Times and Dates* can help you out.

Stay in Top Form!

If you want to stay in top Excel form, consider subscribing to *ExcelTips*. Your subscription is free; all you need is an e-mail account and you can receive a weekly dose of tips related to Excel. To subscribe, just visit the *ExcelTips* Web site:

`http://excel.tips.net`

If you prefer to only consider tips that work with Excel 2007 or Excel 2010, then you'll want to visit our website that focuses on those versions:

`http://excelribbon.tips.net`

ExcelTips is part of the Tips.Net network, a collection of websites designed to bring you helpful tips, tricks, and ideas that can save you time, effort, and money. You can see the full breadth of the Tips.Net network by visiting our website:

`http://www.tips.net`

Visit http://store.tips.net for more great Tips.Net titles!

Made in United States
Orlando, FL
04 November 2026

90200520R00120